CAREERS IN DEMAND FOR HIGH SCHOOL GRADUATES

Armed Forces

Daniel Lewis

MASON CREST

Mason Crest
450 Parkway Drive, Suite D
Broomall, PA 19008
www.masoncrest.com

Printed in the United States of America
First printing
9 8 7 6 5 4 3 2 1

Series ISBN: 978-1-4222-4132-5
Hardcover ISBN: 978-1-4222-4133-2

Library of Congress Cataloging-in-Publication Data is available on file.

Developed and Produced by Print Matters Productions, Inc.
(www.printmattersinc.com)
Cover and Interior Design by TK

CAREERS IN DEMAND FOR HIGH SCHOOL GRADUATES

Agriculture, Food & Natural Resources

Armed Forces

Computers, Communications & the Arts

Construction & Trades

Fitness, Personal Care Services & Education

Health Care & Science

Hospitality & Human Services

Public Safety & Law

Sales, Marketing & Finance

Transportation & Manufacturing

KEY ICONS TO LOOK FOR:

Words to understand: These words with their easy-to-understand definitions will increase the reader's understanding of the text while building vocabulary skills.

Sidebars: This boxed material within the main text allows readers to build knowledge, gain insights, explore possibilities, and broaden their perspectives by weaving together additional information to provide realistic and holistic perspectives.

Educational Videos: Readers can view videos by scanning our QR codes, providing them with additional educational content to supplement the text. Examples include news coverage, moments in history, speeches, iconic sports moments and much more!

Text-dependent Questions: These questions send the reader back to the text for more careful attention to the evidence presented there.

Research projects: Readers are pointed toward areas of further inquiry connected to each chapter. Suggestions are provided for projects that encourage deeper research and analysis.

CONTENTS

INTRODUCTION

This book, highlighting possible careers with the U.S. armed forces, differs from the other volumes in the Careers in Demand for High School Graduates series. Quite simply, enlisting in the military is not the same as working in the civilian world, even if the job descriptions match. That's because joining the military is an enormous commitment.

Most first-term enlistments require a commitment to four years of active duty and two years of inactive duty. It is very hard to get out of the military if you change your mind after you join. You cannot simply quit, and the U.S. armed forces considers it a crime for you to leave your unit or disobey an order. A recruiter might tell you that you can try out the military and get out after just six months if you do not care for it. This is not really true. There is no such thing as an honorable discharge for "failure to adjust" in the military. What's more, planners at the Pentagon can decide to extend your tour of duty, so you may not get out when you think you will. You need to weigh any potential benefits of joining the armed forces against the fact that, once you sign up, you are not entirely in control of your own life anymore. If you can deal with this and you're still interested, read on.

The armed forces is divided into five branches: U.S. Army, Marine Corps, U.S. Navy, U.S. Air Force, and the Coast Guard. All branches except the Coast Guard are part of the Department of Defense. The Coast Guard, which is the smallest of the branches, became part of the Department of Homeland Security in 2003, but it still operates under the Department of Defense in time of war.

As of 2017, there were more than 1.2 million people serving on active duty in the U.S. military. An additional 1.1 million were in the reserves.

The U.S. armed forces is a voluntary military. That means that there is no conscription (draft), and no one is forced to serve. Because of this, the military constantly has to recruit the people to fill its many positions. You've seen the advertisements. They promise job training, money for college, adventure, and leadership skills. It is crucial to remember, however, that military recruiters are basically salespeople. Their job is to convince you to enlist. Most recruiters have to sign up a certain quota of people each month in order to advance their careers. During periods when joining the military is not a popular option, such as when the United States is fighting a war, the pressure on recruiters intensifies. In those times, recruiters stress the benefits of military service and place less emphasis on the drawbacks.

Total Active Duty Personnel (as of August 2017)

Service	Total personnel	Percentage of total force	Percentage female
Army	452,064	37.8	13.2
Marine Corps	178,213	13.9	6.2
Navy	275,296	22.9	15
Air Force	258,095	22.6	11.6
Coast Guard	33,228	2.9	14

On the one hand, there are real benefits to joining the military, including the following:

- **Job training** The military offers thousands of specialized jobs in a wide variety of fields. You don't have to be in the infantry. The majority of military jobs have direct civilian counterparts, and most of these are noncombat occupations. Of course, the numbers don't tell the whole story. That's because, according to the military, all positions are potentially combat positions. However, the current ratio of combat to noncombat troops (also called the "tooth to tail ratio") is roughly about 1:3.

- **Educational benefits** The U.S. armed forces offer excellent educational benefits. After your tour of enlistment is over, a program called the Montgomery GI Bill provides financial support for you to continue your education. The amount that the U.S. government will provide to offset education costs depends on a number of factors, including the length of your enlistment, the type of education or training you're getting, whether or not you have dependents, and whether you are attending full time or part time. But generally speaking, support ranges in the neighborhood of $1,000 to $2,000 per month.

- **Fringe benefits** As a member of the military, you get free medical and dental care, free gym and exercise facilities, free on-base housing (if available), and 30 days of vacation with pay.

- **Travel** Moving on is a way of life in the military. You might be sent somewhere in the United States or perhaps anywhere around the world. A popular U.S. Navy recruiting slogan remains, "Join the navy—see the world."

- **Career** In the military, you earn a steady paycheck from the moment you sign up. If you join at age 18, you can serve a full 20 years and retire at age 38!

- **Sense of purpose** As a member of the U.S. armed forces, you are part of an organization that is important in the world. You're not working just to make money and acquire more consumer junk. Ideally, you're helping to defend the national security of the United States.

On the other hand, there are definite disadvantages to joining the U.S. armed forces. The first drawback is obvious; you may be killed or seriously injured. Similarly, you may have to kill someone else whom you don't know and with whom you don't have a personal quarrel. In some eras, this was a remote possibility. In others, such as during the Vietnam War or the Gulf Wars in Iraq, the chances increased dramatically. The main purpose of the military is to fight; if you want the benefits, you may have to walk the walk.

In addition, the military is not for every type of personality, especially if you have trouble following orders. The U.S. armed forces is rigidly hierarchical, and respect for the authority of all higher-ranking people is a core principle. As a member, you have to assume and trust that higher-ranking people are acting in your (and the nation's) best interest. If the United States goes to war, you have to fight regardless of your personal views. Once you enlist, you can't choose whether to take up arms.

Before you decide to enlist, look carefully at what you will actually be doing. Jobs with fancy-sounding titles often hide low-skill and nontechnical positions. Some military jobs are so different from their civilian counterparts that you may have to be retrained after you leave the military. Most important, the military is not required to keep you full time in the job for which you trained. Nor do they have to keep you in it for the entire time you are in the military. Keep in mind as well that some advanced training programs require additional service commitments or additional active duty time.

If you do not like to travel, the armed forces is probably not for you. Military units in all services can be deployed away from home ports, bases, or airfields at any time. As of 2015, the United States occupied nearly 800 military bases in more than 70 countries and territories around the world.

It's true that joining the military is a way to "serve your country." However, it is not the only way, and it is not unpatriotic to pass on military service. Fighting fires or helping students in an inner city aids the country as much as driving a forklift on an airbase in Germany. The ultimate value of military service is a judgment only each individual can make for him or herself. This does not mean you shouldn't enlist. But you should only enlist if you are sure this is the right choice for you. Your decision will affect your own life, the lives of your family members, and, possibly, the lives of many other people.

If you do decide to enlist, don't sign any papers until you take them home for a parent, teacher, or someone else you trust to review them. When you enlist, you sign an enlistment contract. This contract determines your initial commitment, signing bonuses, job-training guarantees, and any other incentives. Make absolutely sure to get all the recruiter's promises in writing in your enlistment agreement. No oral agreement you made with the recruiter is binding; it has to be in writing. Find out whether you need to pass a special test, get a security clearance, or do anything else before you can get the job or options you want.

Remember, there are slightly different enlistment requirements for each branch. However, minimum entrance age requirements for the U.S. armed forces are a standard 17 years of age with parental consent or 18 years of age without parental consent.

Physical requirements for each branch of the service also vary and can differ even within a branch for various subcategories of troops. In general, enlistees should be in good physical condition, of appropriate weight, and able to pass a standard physical screening prior to entry. If you report to basic training too out of shape to train with the others, you may be placed in a separate remedial physical fitness program. Spare yourself the embarrassment and make sure you're in decent shape beforehand.

You have a better chance of getting your military job of choice if you have a high school diploma. Candidates with a credential of general educational development (GED) can enlist, but some services may limit their opportunities. Without a high school diploma or equivalent, you're more than likely bound for the infantry or a similarly unskilled position.

After you enlist, you will be sent for some form of "basic training," as the U.S. Army calls it. Terminology for all training tends to vary from branch to branch. Of course, enlistees have their own choice words for it. Basic training is a rough program of physical and mental training required to join the military. It is carried out at several different bases around the United States. Basic training can last anywhere from nine weeks to more than one year, depending on the career a person chooses on enlistment. Despite its reputation for difficulty, about 90 percent of recruits successfully complete basic training.

What You Need to Qualify for the Branches of the Armed Services

To join the . . .	You must:
Air Force	Be between the ages of 17 and 27.* Have no more than two dependents. Take the Armed Services Vocational Aptitude Battery test (ASVAB). (Minimum Armed Forces Qualification Test Score: 50)
Army	Be between the ages of 17 and 34.* Have no more than two dependents. Take the Armed Services Vocational Aptitude Battery test. (Minimum Armed Forces Qualification Test Score: 31)
Coast Guard	Be between the ages of 17 and 39.* Have no more than two dependents. Take the Armed Services Vocational Aptitude Battery test. (Minimum Armed Forces Qualification Test Score: 45) Have a willingness to serve on or around the water.

Marines	Be between the ages of 17 and 29.* Take the Armed Forces Qualification Test. (Minimum Armed Forces Qualification Test Score: 32) Meet "exacting" physical and moral standards.
Navy	Be between the ages of 17 and 34.* Take the Armed Forces Qualification Test. (Minimum Armed Forces Qualification Test Score: 50)

* Allowable age range may vary, depending on additional factors, such as previous service and training.

Advanced Individual Training (AIT), another army term, makes up the rest of the training period. In the AIT (again, the terminology varies from branch to branch), recruits train to become experts in their chosen field (sometimes known as "military occupational specialty," or "MOS"). Therefore, the length of AIT differs depending on what specialty you select. If an individual chooses to enlist as a food service specialist, then some of his or her AIT would be spent at the U.S. Army Quartermaster Center and School at Fort Lee, Virginia. However, a person who chooses law enforcement and security would probably train at Fort Leonard Wood in Missouri, home of the Military Police School. In general, each branch has its own advanced individual training programs. Although advanced training schools do not center on combat, enlistees are still subject to the same duties, strict daily schedule, and disciplinary rules as in basic training.

The range of possible military careers is quite broad, and it would take an extremely long book to cover all of them. This volume highlights careers in the U.S. armed forces that are available at an entry level with only a high school diploma. Some of these jobs will be familiar, and others unfamiliar. The book attempts to cover a fairly wide range of specialties to give you a feeling for the range of possibilities of military enlistment. Don't forget that most of these jobs are available in at least four of the five branches and that they might differ somewhat from branch to branch.

Some of these military specialties, such as personnel specialist or law enforcement and security specialist, require relatively little academic study. Others, such as aircraft mechanic or medical service technician, require extensive training. Many military careers are becoming increasingly complex. However, the benefit of joining the military is that you don't need to spend four years in a classroom to learn these job skills. Instead, you can learn them on the job.

If you are reading this book, you understand that pursuing something besides a college degree after high school makes sense for many people. College is expensive, and costs continue to rise much faster than inflation. Many individuals cannot afford the thousands of dollars needed to get a degree. The U.S. military offer programs with two-, three-, and six-year active duty, or reserve enlistments. It depends upon the branch and the job that you want. For the right person, it is a viable alternative to college.

There is a wide range of exciting and satisfying military careers available without a college diploma. In addition, there is no rule that says that you can't go back to college later in life, in five, ten, or even twenty years. In most cases, the military will help defray at least part of the cost. If you can deal with the commitment and the mission, then perhaps this is the route for you.

◀ **Before you make the decision to join the U.S. armed forces, it is important to sit with a recruiter to discuss your options and whether it is right for you.**

1

Construction Equipment Operator

Construct dams and buildings. Drive and control bulldozers, graders, and other heavy equipment. Build and maintain roads and airfields.

WORDS TO UNDERSTAND

crawler tractor: a type of construction equipment that moves on tracks instead of wheels.

efficiency: productivity; working without wasted effort.

pneumatic: a tool that's operated by air under pressure.

When you were young, did you get a kick out of playing with toy dump trucks and tractors? Does the idea of operating heavy equipment still fascinate you? Each year, the U.S. armed forces completes hundreds of building and maintenance projects around the world. Military workers move tons of earth to construct airfields, roads, dams, and buildings. They deliver building materials to a site and then place them in the proper position. These are all tasks that require construction equipment operators. These specialists drive bulldozers, graders, and other heavy equipment to cut and level earth for runways and roadbeds. They also operate smaller equipment, such as air compressors and pneumatic tools. The job is a dream come true for people who loved to play with toy vehicles and machines as kids.

◀ **A pavements and construction journeyman sweeps away gravel at Eielson Air Force Base, Alaska.**

▲ **Air Force civil engineers and U.S. Army combat heavy engineers work together, laying mortar on structural blocks. They are building a primary school in Belize as a part of a construction project called New Horizons.**

Is This Job Right for You?

Would working as a construction equipment operator be a good fit for you? To find out, read each of the following questions and answer "Yes" or "No."

Yes	***No***	**1.** *Do you like to work outdoors?*
Yes	***No***	**2.** *Do you enjoy a job that allows you to use your hands?*
Yes	***No***	**3.** *Are you interested in operating construction equipment?*
Yes	***No***	**4.** *Do you like to build things?*
Yes	***No***	**5.** *Do you have a good sense of balance?*
Yes	***No***	**6.** *Are you detail oriented?*
Yes	***No***	**7.** *Do you like tinkering with machines?*
Yes	***No***	**8.** *Can you work under conditions that may be noisy and uncomfortable?*
Yes	***No***	**9.** *Are you in good physical condition?*
Yes	***No***	**10.** *Do you have good hand–eye–foot coordination?*

If you answered "Yes" to most of these questions, you might consider a career as a construction equipment operator. To find out more about this job, read on.

What's the Work Like?

As a military construction equipment operator, you will repair or build structures. You will use any of many different machines, both large and small, to construct airfields, dams, bridges, roads, and buildings. You might operate trucks, bulldozers, backhoes, forklifts, pile-drivers, graders, or cranes to clear and grade land and prepare it for construction. You might operate a **crawler tractor** to construct embankments and excavate hills and slopes, or you might use it for cleaning, stripping, backfilling, stockpiling, or pushing a scraper.

TALKING MONEY

Compensation in the military is primarily based on years of service. A private with less than two years in the armed forces draws a base income of about $19,000 annually, whereas a corporal with four years' service earns about $29,000 per year. Government benefits are famously excellent and include career training, health care, some money for college, and life insurance. Most soldiers on active duty also receive further compensation. In civilian life, construction equipment operators have a mean annual salary of $45,000, according to 2016 data from the U.S. Bureau of Labor Statistics.

Other commonly used machines include control power shovels, which are used to dig holes and trenches to lay or repair sewer and other pipelines. Excavation and loading machines equipped with scoops, shovels, or buckets are operated to dig sand, gravel, and earth and load it into trucks. You could use winches, cranes, and hoists to lift and move heavy construction materials.

General construction equipment operators use air compressors, pumps, and **pneumatic** tools. They also operate specialized construction machines that pump, compact, ditch, and augur. And don't forget that the heavy construction equipment itself needs to be transported to and from a site using a tractor-trailer.

Another area of construction is paving roads or airfields using asphalt or concrete. Tamping equipment operators run machines that compact earth and other materials for roadbeds. Concrete-paving machine operators control machines that spread, vibrate,

▲ **An airman with a civil engineer squadron flattens a section of new asphalt with a steam roller at a base in South Carolina.**

and level wet concrete in forms. They use other attachments to smooth the surface of the concrete, spray on a curing compound, and cut expansion joints. Construction equipment operation is a huge field with many choices, both in and out of the military.

Who's Hiring?

- All five service branches use construction equipment operators.
- Construction and maintenance units. Military construction equipment operators often work in specific units.

- The Seabees. The Seabees, founded during World War II, are the construction units of the U.S. Navy. They have built hundreds of bases and bulldozed and paved thousands of miles of roadway and airstrips. Their unofficial motto is "Can Do!"

Where Are the Jobs?

Most military construction equipment operators work outdoors. They often get muddy, dusty, or greasy while working in nearly every type of climate and weather condition. Military operations cannot stop just because it is scorching hot, freezing cold, or sopping wet. For example, you might have to remove ice and snow from runways, roads, and other northern or mountainous areas using scrapers and snow blowers. This means operators will be chilled in the winter and overheated in the summer. However, operators might occasionally work indoors while repairing equipment.

TALKING TRENDS

In civilian life, construction is one of the nation's largest industries. It employs more than 9 million people; about 420,000 of them operate construction equipment. The job market in civilian construction obviously depends on the economy. However, employment is expected to increase with population and business growth. Prospects for military workers will be steady as long as there is money for the services, although the trend toward the military using private contractors for big projects may reduce employment over time.

Some operators work in remote locations—such as Iceland, Guam, or Turkey—on large construction projects like highways and dams, or in factory or mining operations. The U.S. armed forces is involved all around the world, and you might be sent anywhere. Be prepared to move.

Operators may work irregular hours because work on some construction projects continues around the clock. Construction work might have to be performed late at night or early in the morning. This is especially true if you are involved in working in a combat zone. In general, however, construction equipment operation works a standard schedule.

A Typical Day

Here are some highlights for a typical day as a construction equipment operator working with asphalt.

Consult with the mixing plant to make asphalt. Mixing the asphalt correctly is very important. Without the asphalt mixed in the proper proportions, a crew could not build a quality roadway. You assist the hot-plant operator to make sure the proper mix is produced.

▲ A U.S. Air Force staff sergeant spreads gravel in front of a new fitness center at Nellis Air Force Base.

Transport the asphalt to the site. You are in charge of transferring the 300-degree-Fahrenheit asphalt from the silo to the site. You wear personal protective equipment and watch out for burns, spills, falls, explosions, and overfills.

Spread the asphalt. To build the road, the asphalt has to be dumped, spread, and leveled. You operate the paving machine to control the temperature and flow of asphalt onto the roadbed. You make sure that the asphalt-paving machine distributes the paving material evenly and doesn't leave empty spaces.

Start Preparing Now

- Take relevant classes in high school. Helpful subjects include automobile and shop mechanics, science, and mechanical drawing.
- Take a class at a vocational school. Vocational schools often teach the operation of some types of construction equipment. Completion of such programs, or even a class, gives an applicant a definite advantage when it comes to getting the specialty requested.
- Get some real experience. Experience operating related equipment, such as farm tractors or heavy equipment, is a huge asset.

Training and How to Get It

Job training for a military construction equipment operator begins with about nine weeks of basic training. In basic training, recruits learn basic soldiering skills. This is followed by four to 12 weeks of advanced individual training, depending on the job classification. You'll spend part of this time in the classroom and part in the field.

In the classroom, you'll learn about the operation of different types of construction equipment and vehicles. You might specialize in one type of machine in the armed forces, but you also might have to know how to operate several different types. You will also learn how to set up and inspect the equipment, make mechanical adjustments, and perform some maintenance and minor repairs.

However, construction equipment operators usually learn most of their skills on the job. You'll probably start by operating light equipment while an experienced operator looks on. Later you may operate heavier equipment, such as bulldozers and cranes.

NOTES FROM THE FIELD

Structural specialist, *vertical repair shop, Bolling Air Force Base, Washington, D.C.*

Q: *How did you get your job?*

A: My dad was in the air force for four years and talked about it a lot. I decided to give the air force a chance. I planned on being in the service for four years, but now I've been in for 12 years and have established a career. I'm also close to finishing my associate's degree in construction technology.

When I came into the air force, I was young, active, and athletic. I wanted to work outside and work with my hands. By the time that I finished basic training, they had combined some career fields, so at tech school I also learned carpentry, masonry, welding, and sheet metal work. My first assignment [included] a lot of facility maintenance but I was eager to do more major construction work. A senior airman suggested that I volunteer for an overseas assignment to gain more experience. I ended up going to Okinawa [Japan] for six years.

Q: *What do you like best about your job?*

A: My best experience was in Honduras, where we were part of a humanitarian mission and built a maternity clinic in the poor town of Jutiapa . . . I [especially like the] travel and career opportunities.

Q: *What's the most challenging part of your job?*

A: I was in Iraq in 2003 and did site survey work for the National Intelligence Center (NIC). It was the early stage of the Iraq war, and they needed everything from communication lines to basic power. We were living out of one of the palaces and I rigged up an air conditioning unit, using formica and duct tape to make duct work.

Q: *What are the keys to success to being a construction equipment operator?*

A: In addition to the construction and managerial skills that I've developed in the air force, I've also learned the importance of teamwork. In many situations, your life is on the line, so teamwork is essential.

The operation of construction equipment is becoming more complicated. Technologically advanced construction equipment uses computerized controls and complex hydraulics and electronics. Global Positioning System (GPS) technology now helps with grading and leveling activities. These newer machines require more skill to operate. If you plan to operate this type of equipment, you may need additional training and some understanding of electronics.

Watch military road-builders in action.

▲ An Air Force Reserve tech demonstrates a heavy equipment simulator. Simulators like these are used to provide initial qualification and upgrade training for heavy equipment operators while providing a safer learning environment for trainees.

You can apply most of the training you receive in the military to credit hours toward a college degree. You might also have the opportunity for continued education through various college programs or tuition assistance. There are several three-year apprenticeship programs for which you may qualify. These programs, run by the International Union of Operating Engineers and the Associated General Contractors of America, consist of at least three years or 6,000 hours of on-the-job training and 144 hours per year of classroom instruction.

All of these skills are easily transferred to the civilian job market if you want to do so. Whether in the military or the civilian world, construction equipment operators use their combined **efficiency**, teamwork, and reliability to build almost anything in any place.

Learn the Lingo

Here are a few words you'll hear in this career:

- **Backfill** The replacement of excavated earth into a trench around and against a basement foundation.
- **Backhoe** A backhoe is a self-powered excavation machine that digs by pulling a boom-mounted bucket toward itself. A backhoe digs foundations and footings and helps install drainage or sewer systems.
- **Pile driver** A large machine, mounted on skids, barges, or cranes, that hammers piles into the ground. Piles are long, heavy beams of wood or steel driven into the ground to support retaining walls, piers, or building foundations.

Finding a Job

Many young men and women enlist in the armed forces right out of high school. For an 18-year-old graduate, the step consists of nothing more than paying a visit to the local armed forces recruiting office.

To serve in the U.S. military, a person must pass physical requirements and a background check. For the army, your service obligations would be determined at the recruiter's office.

You can agree with the recruiter to serve for two, three, four, or even five years. Job specialties are subject to availability and an applicant's qualifications. As with all jobs, some previous experience in the field will move you toward the head of the list.

Tips for Success

- Be willing to travel. Many construction equipment operator jobs involve traveling around the world with the U.S. armed forces. Some people prefer this type of life with its frequent moves, others do not.
- Practice makes perfect. Volunteer with the local parks department to get experience working with machines.

Reality Check

Operating construction equipment is a little like driving a car. It is exciting at first but may grow tedious after a time. So imagine driving a bulldozer for your career. You will be sitting for long periods of time. Heavy machinery is noisy and shakes or jolts the operator. Operating it can also be dangerous.

Some Other Jobs to Think About

Truck driver; agricultural equipment operator. These civilian careers offer the opportunity to operate heavy mechanical equipment outside of the construction industry. Truck drivers are also needed by the U.S. armed forces.

Carpenter, electrician, plumber. These jobs are all construction positions that do not usually involve the operation of large mechanical equipment. They're perfect for people who like to build things.

Automobile mechanic. An excellent job for problem solvers who enjoy tinkering with machines.

How to Move Up

- Advance in the military. In the armed forces, promotions can come quickly based on time in service and merit. After four years, you can become a crew leader. Among other duties, these officers oversee teams of construction specialists. They interpret drawings and blueprints to plan and lay out work. After 19 years, you can advance to "trades superintendent." Trades superintendents supervise large construction and maintenance units.
- Advance in civilian life. The ability to operate several different types of construction equipment makes you more valuable and is usually a step to higher pay. This may require taking some extra classes at a vocational school. Beyond this, operators move to crew leaders or contractors. The construction skills that you learn in the armed forces, in addition to leadership training, will help advance your career. The majority of civilian equipment operators work for the construction industry; other employers include state or local governments and mining, manufacturing, or utility companies.

LEARN MORE ONLINE

CAREERS IN THE MILITARY

This Web site is the starting point for any investigation of jobs in the armed forces. It includes many useful job descriptions and links. http://www.careersinthemilitary.com

TODAY'S MILITARY

This site gives in-depth information on each branch of the U.S. armed forces. http://www.todaysmilitary.com

NATIONAL CENTER FOR CONSTRUCTION EDUCATION AND RESEARCH.

The center is an education foundation affiliated with the University of Florida. The Web site has useful information about training and safety programs. https://www.nccer.org/nccer-home

TEXT-DEPENDENT QUESTIONS

1. ***How do you get trained for this field?***
2. ***What is a backhoe?***
3. ***What are some related jobs you might consider?***

RESEARCH PROJECTS

1. *If you are 16 or older, you can look for a summer construction job. If you know anyone who works in the field, start by asking them if they are hiring. If not, try your state labor department's Web site, which may list upcoming job postings. You can also check on sites like www.myfirstpaycheck.com and www.snagajob.com, which are focused on helping teens find work.*

2. *Read this article about the daily life of a construction officer in the Navy (http://todaysmilitary.com/profile-steve-opalinek-facilities-officer). Consider if his life is one that would suit you.*

▲ The construction experience gained in the military will prepare you for good jobs when you get out.

CLOSE
A1
S1
S2

Electrical Equipment Repairer

2

Use cutting-edge technology. Solve challenging problems. Fix broken electrical equipment.

WORDS TO UNDERSTAND

altimeter: an instrument that registers changes in atmospheric pressure to measure altitude.

apprentice: a trainee who performs hands-on work to learn a particular skill.

circuit: here, a completely closed path along which electricity can flow.

superintendent: someone who oversees a large operation, such as a construction superintendent.

Electricity powers most of the equipment used by the U.S. armed forces. Whether it's a vehicle or a machine, chances are that electrical equipment repairers fix, maintain, or inspect it. Electric motors, electric tools, and medical equipment need precision maintenance and repair. The world's most advanced weaponry, ships, and aircraft could not operate without electricity. All of these systems need to be maintained by servicemen and -women to enable the military to function. If you are fascinated by circuits, electrical work, and electronics, then electrical equipment repair might be the field for you.

◀ **An electrician in the Electrical Overhaul Support Branch works on a power distribution box assembly.**

Is This Job Right for You?

Would working as an electrical equipment repairer be a good fit for you? To find out, read each of the following questions and answer "Yes" or "No."

Yes	***No***	**1.**	*Do you like to work with your hands?*
Yes	***No***	**2.**	*Do you like doing physical work?*
Yes	***No***	**3.**	*Could you see yourself confidently working on multimillion dollar machinery?*
Yes	***No***	**4.**	*Are you interested in how electrical equipment works?*
Yes	***No***	**5.**	*Do you work accurately, and with attention to detail?*
Yes	***No***	**6.**	*Are you confident enough to work with high-voltage electricity?*
Yes	***No***	**7.**	*Are you mechanically inclined?*
Yes	***No***	**8.**	*Are you a good problem solver?*
Yes	***No***	**9.**	*Do you enjoy studying math and shop mechanics in school?*
Yes	***No***	**10.**	*Do you keep your cool under pressure?*

If you answered "Yes" to most of these questions, you might consider a career as an electrical equipment repairer. To find out more about this job, read on.

What's the Work Like?

The field of electrical repair is so large that it almost defies a job description. The military uses electricity to do countless jobs, including lighting hospitals, running power tools, and operating computers. In addition, every military base, no matter where in the world, has its own electrical supply. This creates thousands of jobs for military electricians.

As an electrical equipment repairer, you would be responsible for repairing electrical systems in offices, repair shops, airplane hangars, ships, and other buildings. When breakdowns occur, you

TALKING MONEY

Military jobs pay according to seniority, with privates and corporals—with two and four years' service, respectively—earning base salaries of between $19,000 and $29,000 per year. Military benefits include career training, health care, money for college, and life insurance. In civilian life, electricians have annual average earnings of more than $52,720, according to 2016 data from the U.S. Bureau of Labor Statistics.

would make the necessary repairs as quickly as possible in order to reduce inconvenience and protect the integrity of the facility. You might have to replace items or install new circuit breakers, fuses, switches, or wire. Then you would test the repair to make sure the system was operational and safe.

However, because electricity is so widely used in the armed forces, there are hundreds of other possibilities with regard to your duties. You may routinely inspect, maintain, and repair some of the most technologically advanced communications, navigation, and combat-systems equipment in the world. Alternatively, you might be fixing portable electric tools, such as saws and drills. Much depends on your training and area of expertise.

Some of your work might be specific to the military. You might have to repair devices such as night-vision equipment or battlefield illumination devices. You might also study the electrical systems aboard a Seahawk helicopter. Someone has to repair the nuclear, biological, and chemical warning and measuring devices. You might even be fixing the complex electrical systems for guided missiles and their launching systems.

▲ **An aviation electrician's mate troubleshoots a blade-folding issue on a Seahawk helicopter.**

However, a great deal of the job is the standard electrical work that transfers easily to the civilian world. You would repair electric motors, generators, switchboards, and control equipment as well as power and lighting **circuits** and electrical fixtures. You may also inspect and repair electrical, medical, and dental equipment, as well as instruments such as voltmeters, temperature gauges, and **altimeters**. You would read blueprints, manuals, and technical diagrams to locate damaged parts of generators and control equipment and repair them. Whatever you work on, the job of an electrical equipment repairer requires excellent problem-solving skills and technical ability.

Who's Hiring?

- All five branches need electrical equipment repairers.
- The Seabees. This navy construction battalion provides the crucial link between land and naval forces by constructing buildings, ports, and other structures required for ships, aircraft, machinery, and personnel.

Where Are the Jobs?

Because of the common need for electrical services, electrical equipment repairers can be found in all parts of the military and all over the world. For example, you might work in a repair shop aboard a ship, on a military base in the United States, or at an airfield in a combat zone.

Electrical equipment repairers work both indoors and outdoors. Repair work has to happen regardless of the weather. This means you may be working in the 110-degree sun or in below-zero temperatures. The work can sometimes be strenuous. You might have to lift heavy objects and stand, stoop, and kneel for long periods.

Most electricians work a standard 40-hour week, although you may have to work additional hours

TALKING TRENDS

Anything with wiring, gears, or other parts eventually breaks down. Electricians held almost 630,000 jobs in 2016, and the Bureau of Labor Statistics projects that employment in the field should increase by as much as 14 percent through the year 2024. One key area of growth is alternative power, where an increasing number of electricians will be needed.

▲ **An air force airman tightens wiring underneath an F-15 Eagle during a mission employment phase exercise on Nellis Air Force Base.**

for major projects. You may have to work nights, weekends, and holidays. You may also spend time on call, ready to drop whatever you're doing and race to the worksite.

A Typical Day

Here are some highlights for a typical day as an electrical equipment repairer (or "electrician's mate") aboard a U.S. Coast Guard cutter.

Perform scheduled maintenance. A great deal of your job will be performing routine but tedious tasks. This morning, you repair a sound-powered telephone.

Be a jack-of-all-trades. You stand watch in the engine room to gain broad experience in all aspects of engineering. However, you're called on to emergency-troubleshoot a glitch in the aircraft landing/takeoff equipment. As the only electrical specialist on board, you're often expected to handle very complex tasks such as this one.

See what it's like to be a military electrician.

Work with civilian technical assistants. In the afternoon, you shift gears to work with technically advanced equipment, such as the glide slope indicator and the gyro compasses. You brainstorm solutions with civilian technical assistants—an outstanding training and educational experience.

Start Preparing Now

- Take relevant high school courses. Helpful school subjects include math, electricity and electronics, and shop mechanics.
- Enroll in a course at a community college. Taking classes demonstrates your interest and seriousness. It will also help you get your requested specialty.
- Work as a helper. You can learn many electrical skills this way. A helper assists electricians in setting up job sites, gathering materials, and doing other nonelectrical work. Look up opportunities on area job boards and ask around.
- Become an **apprentice**. This is not easy to do—and if you can get into an apprenticeship program, you may no longer want to join the military. However, this is the time-honored way to learn electrical skills.

Training and How to Get It

Job training for an electrical equipment repairer in the armed forces consists of nine weeks of basic training in which you will learn basic soldiering skills. If you successfully complete basic training, there are another 6 to 26 weeks of advanced individual training. Part of this training will take place in the classroom and part in on-the-job training. The amount of training you will receive depends on your specialty.

NOTES FROM THE FIELD

Electronics repair technician,
Norfolk Naval Shipyard, Norfolk, Virginia

Q: *How did you get your job?*

A: **When I first graduated from high school, I had never considered joining the military. I wanted to get out of the house, get a job, and go to college. After [two years of] struggling to pay rent and tuition, I . . . decided to enter the navy—in a technical field, because I liked the educational options that went along with enlistment. I also knew technical skills would be in demand after I left the military. After some initial training, I had the opportunity to specialize in the electronics field. I decided to become an electronics technician because the big companies are always looking for those people.**

Q: *What do you like best about your job?*

A: **I . . . was impressed by the amount of preparation I received for my first tour. . . . [It] was an unbelievable experience. I'm planning to finish college using the navy's tuition assistance programs, and I hope to become an officer one day.**

Q: *What's the most challenging part of your job?*

A: **[When I was] aboard the USS *Puget Sound* in the Mediterranean Sea, I repaired calibration and test equipment that was used to analyze the electronic components and systems on the ship, such as communications, radar and sonar, navigation, and electronic warfare systems. . . . On the USS *Wasp*, I was responsible for insuring that the electronic systems were operating properly before the ship went on an extended cruise.**

Q: *What are the keys to success to being an electronics repair technician?*

A: **Aboard ship—everybody must become a jack-of-all-trades!**

In the classroom, you will cover basic electrical system maintenance and repair procedures. This includes topics such as the basic principles of electricity and electronics, electrical circuit troubleshooting, soldering techniques, and the proper procedure for wiring switches, outlets, and junction boxes. Of course, you will also study safety procedures in some detail.

In the field, you will work with an experienced electrician to practice the installation and repair of electrical wiring systems and electrical products. At first, you will just drill holes, set anchors, and attach wiring. Later, you'll install, connect, and test wiring, outlets, and switches. Finally, you will learn techniques to troubleshoot communications systems and to install, maintain, and repair sophisticated computerized equipment.

Your training in the U.S. armed forces will teach you more than just electrical repair. More important, you will learn teamwork skills and attention to detail. The training you will receive in this field can often be used toward a bachelor's or associate's degree. You may also receive an opportunity for continued education through various military college programs, in addition to tuition assistance.

Learn the Lingo

Here are a few words you'll hear in this career:

- **Ape** Slang for an "auxiliary power unit" (or APU). This is a small turbine engine on an aircraft that is started with a battery. It then supplies electrical power for starting the main engines.
- **GFCI** or **GFI** An abbreviation for "ground fault circuit interrupter." This is a type of circuit protection usually required in kitchens and bathrooms. It helps safeguard against shocks.
- **Twidget** Nickname for a sailor in the electrical field.
- **Uninterruptible power supply (UPS)** A UPS device provides a constant supply of power, even if there are interruptions to the normal power supply. It is usually used with computer equipment.

Finding a Job

Many young men and women enlist in the armed forces right out of high school. If you're 18 years old, all you have to do is visit a local recruiting office. Seventeen-year-olds can also enlist but need a parent's permission.

To serve in the U.S. military, a person must pass physical requirements and a background check. Academically, an applicant must score at least a 31 on the Armed Forces Qualification Test (AFQT). For the army, your service obligations would be determined at the recruiter's office. (Read the fine print carefully to understand your possible length of service or number of tours.)

▲ **Members of a civil engineer squadron work to restore power at Scott Air Force Base.**

Tips for Success

- Develop your troubleshooting skills. To be an electrical equipment repairer, it helps to be able to read blueprints, wiring plans, and repair orders. That's one of the main ways to determine what went wrong with a piece of electrical equipment and how to fix it.
- Listen to what people are saying. Sometimes the user of a machine may know more about its behavior than you think, and may be able to offer useful clues to fixing it.

Reality Check

Electricity is unforgiving of mistakes. Electrical equipment repairers risk injury from electrical shock. Accidents are rare, but they do happen. For instance, in the civilian world, the position of electrical power line repairers is usually ranked in the top 10 of the most dangerous jobs in the United States.

Some Other Jobs to Think About

Machinist. Machinists make, repair, and modify metal and nonmetal parts for engines and other types of machines.

Mechanic. You can still work in the repair field as a mechanic. This job comes with a host of subspecialties, such as aircraft, automobile, electronics, engine, refrigeration, hydroelectric, and radio.

Technical writer. If you like the field but do not want to climb the ladders, then this is a good option. You can write or rewrite complex scientific, training, or other professional material for a knowledgeable audience.

LEARN MORE ONLINE

CAREERS IN THE MILITARY

This Web site is the starting point for any investigation of jobs in the armed forces. It includes many useful job descriptions and links. http://www.careersinthemilitary.com

TODAY'S MILITARY

This site gives in-depth information on each branch of the U.S. armed forces. http://www.todaysmilitary.com

INTERNATIONAL BROTHERHOOD OF ELECTRICAL WORKERS

The brotherhood represents about 750,000 electrical workers in a wide variety of fields. This large Web site is a gold mine for information on a career in electrical repair. http://www.ibew.org

How to Move Up

- Advance in the military. In the armed forces, promotions can come quickly, based on time in service and merit. Some jobs within this field offer accelerated promotions to higher pay grades. After four years, you can become a senior repairer, the professional who manages the most complex repair jobs and helps less experienced repairers. After 18 years, you can rise to the level of maintenance superintendent. In this position, you would direct an entire repair facility.

- Advance in civilian life. Electricians usually advance to higher positions based on a combination of experience and extra coursework and passing licensing exams. The National Electrical Code, methods of installation, and the variety of materials are constantly changing. Sometimes, developing a specialty in a field such as low-voltage voice, data, and video systems can be a ticket to higher-paying work. Experienced electricians with enthusiasm and leadership skills can advance to higher-paying positions as supervisor, project manager, construction **superintendent**, or contractor. They can also open their own business or become electrical inspectors.

▲ An electrician's mate uses a flow divider while repairing a forklift battery.

TEXT-DEPENDENT QUESTIONS

1. *What are the responsibilities of an electrical repairer?*
2. *What's an "ape"?*
3. *What are some of the secrets to success in this field?*

RESEARCH PROJECTS

1. *Find out if your school offers courses in electrical repair. You might also be able to start learning about electronics as part of your school's A/V club or even helping out with lights at the drama club. If there is a community college in your neighborhood, you might try there also.*
2. *Read about the history and accomplishments of the Seabees. (http://www.navy.mil/navydata/personnel/seabees/seabee1.html)*

Computer Systems Specialist

3

Troubleshoot and repair broken equipment.
Work with cutting-edge hardware and software.
Install and maintain computer systems.

WORDS TO UNDERSTAND

debugging: testing and fixing problems in computer programs.

mainframe: a large computer that supports a number of workstations.

local area network (LAN): a computer network that connects a group of computers over a small area.

wide area network (WAN): a computer network that covers a large geographic area and may consist of multiple LANs.

If you love computers and want to work with some of the most sophisticated hardware and software available in the world, then a computer systems specialist may be the job for you. The U.S. armed forces is one of the world's largest computer users. The military uses computers to operate equipment during combat and for countless noncombat situations. Computers also manage personnel, logistics, communications, weather systems, and financial information. Computer systems specialists install, operate, and maintain the military's high-tech systems. These, in turn, allow the modern U.S. armed forces to function.

◀ **Computer systems specialists train on a new communications system.**

Is This Job Right for You?

Would working as a computer systems specialist be a good fit for you? To find out, read each of the following questions and answer "Yes" or "No."

Yes **No** 1. *Are you interested in computer and telephone systems?*

Yes **No** 2. *Do you pride yourself on attention to detail?*

Yes **No** 3. *Can you understand and apply math concepts?*

Yes **No** 4. *Do you consider yourself responsible and mature?*

Yes **No** 5. *Can you be trusted with classified information?*

Yes **No** 6. *Would you enjoy working with multimillion dollar technical systems?*

Yes **No** 7. *Do you have good communication skills?*

Yes **No** 8. *Are you interested in solving puzzles and problems?*

Yes **No** 9. *Do you like work that requires attention to detail?*

Yes **No** 10. *Are you well organized?*

If you answered "Yes" to most of these questions, you might consider a career as a computer systems specialist. To find out more about this job, read on.

What's the Work Like?

The job description of computer systems specialists is simple: to maintain, operate, and repair computer equipment. However, there is much more to this field than this streamlined explanation implies. Your most basic duties would be to work on hardware and software installation and maintenance. You would use computers to write programs and collect, enter, and process information. You would also plan, install, and maintain **local area** and **wide area networks** (LANs and WANs).

TALKING MONEY

The federal government pay scale starts low and ends low but includes excellent benefits. Base salary for privates with less than two years of experience is around $19,000. Military benefits include tuition support and health and life insurance. If you qualify as a computer systems specialist, you may be eligible for up to a $40,000 enlistment bonus. Civilian computer systems analysts have median annual earnings of about $87,000, according to 2016 data from the U.S. Bureau of Labor Statistics.

▲ **As a computer systems specialist you will be trained to repair many different machines.**

Working as a computer systems specialist is extremely challenging. You would probably work on a wide variety of state-of-the-art computers, from laptops to **mainframes**, developing, testing, and **debugging** computer programs.

If a computer system or network breaks down, it could be your job to troubleshoot and repair broken equipment. Once a system is working, you might have to perform preventive and corrective maintenance to make sure it stays running. You might also become expert at setting up and taking down computer equipment under field conditions. This might involve working under stress or extreme climate conditions while under enemy fire. You would be working with computers, but you would also be part of the military, so the job could be dangerous.

Computer systems specialists also perform military-specific duties. You might be assigned to detect enemy radar signals and determine their origin. You also might track inbound threats, such as missiles, or operate underwater or satellite telecommunication systems. In many cases, you'd work with highly classified and coded information.

Each branch of the service has its own specific needs. For example, if you work with navy computers, you might have to identify and differentiate sounds produced by ships, submarines, torpedoes, sonar transmissions, marine life, and natural sounds. The job of a computer systems specialist is both wide ranging and challenging.

TALKING TRENDS

Computers help run the modern world. Any training in this field is almost certain to result in a good job. There is a huge demand for people with computer expertise. As a computer systems specialist, you should be able to easily find a position you like in high-tech industry in or out of the military. The Bureau of Labor Statistics estimates that the employment of computer systems analysts is expected to grow much faster than average for all occupations through 2024.

Who's Hiring?

- All major branches of the U.S. military use computer systems specialists.
- The coast guard. Computer systems specialists are stationed throughout the coast guard, including in Alaska and Hawaii. They work out of large and small shops, in shore unit stations, and on all major coast guard cutters.

Where Are the Jobs?

Military computer systems specialists work in offices, laboratories, and computer sites on military bases or aboard ships. You'll usually perform your job in comfortable surroundings and won't have to worry about working outside in the rain. However, you will probably have to sit at a desk for hours at a time. Like other people who spend long periods in front

▲ **The Images-Many-On-Many (IMOMS) computer was used to assess radar threats during Operation Desert Storm.**

of a computer terminal, computer systems specialists may develop eyestrain, backaches, headaches, and hand and wrist problems, such as carpal tunnel syndrome. These are typical concerns for office workers.

Military computer systems specialists typically work about 40 hours a week, the same as many of their peers in civilian life. However, you may have to work longer hours, nights, or weekends in order to meet deadlines, solve specific problems, or help during large-scale military operations.

In some cases, your job could be done from remote locations using laptops, modems, e-mail, and the Internet. However, in most cases you'll probably have to travel to install the system or fix the problem on site.

NOTES FROM THE FIELD

Computer emergency response team,
Information Systems Command, Fort Belvoir, Virginia

Q: ***How did you get your job as a computer systems specialist?***

A: I decided to specialize in computers after six years as an administrative staff member in the army. I switched specialty areas because I saw a great deal of opportunity for people with computer expertise. After my initial training, I performed systems analysis and troubleshooting duties for a financial system at the army's Information Systems Command. I was then posted to Fort Lee, Virginia, where I installed a complex contracting system that would be used at bases all over the world.

Q: ***What do you like best about your job?***

A: [For me, working] on a team installing and maintaining a global command and control system. It was an exciting and hectic time because our mission was to do whatever it took to get the system online.

Q: ***What's the most challenging part of your job?***

A: [It's responding quickly] to computer failures due to everything from natural disasters to intrusions by hackers. I maintain team readiness and ensure that the staff is well trained on the latest technologies.

Q: ***What are the keys to success to being a computer systems specialist?***

A: Teamwork skills . . . [because some projects require you to] work with personnel from all branches of the armed forces.

A Typical Day

Here are some highlights for a typical day as a computer systems specialist for the navy.

Help install a system. A new aircraft carrier has been commissioned for the navy. You're in charge of setting up network administration services, such as e-mail accounts, user training, security, and virus protection.

▲ Computer systems specialists often work remotely with their laptops. Here, a staff sergeant checks computer data at an air force base next to an F-16.

Attend a meeting. Formal and informal get-togethers are common. You might confer about how the navy can use the latest developments in computer software or perhaps discuss ways to defend against hackers.

Fix a breakdown. The computers that control the navigation system aren't working. Is it a hardware or software problem? A virus? Figure it out and fix it—fast!

Start Preparing Now

- Take relevant classes in high school. Helpful school subjects include computer science, math, and keyboarding.
- Experiment with your own computer. There is no substitute for hands-on experience. You have to like playing around with computers to get involved in this field.
- Get some experience. There are all sorts of jobs for people with computer skills. Any practical experience or previous training in telephone or computer systems maintenance and repair will help you break into this specialty.

Training and How to Get It

Job training for a computer systems specialist in the armed forces consists of about nine weeks of basic training, during which you will learn basic soldiering skills. That is followed by 10 to 25 weeks of broad classroom instruction in the operation, maintenance, and repair of computers. You will study computer concepts as well as planning, designing, and testing computer systems. Classroom training includes instruction on computer processors, power supplies, network systems, displays, and printers. You will focus on how each item operates and develop troubleshooting techniques. The length of your job training depends on the specialty area.

You will also receive further on-the-job training and advanced courses in specific computer systems and current programming languages. Because security is so important to the military, an important part of your training will cover computer security issues, coding, and debugging. Working with computers is one of the most security-sensitive jobs in the entire armed forces.

As a computer systems specialist, you will also need a great deal of knowledge of electrical theory. Computer systems specialists sometimes have the responsibility to manage, repair, maintain, and install telephone systems and network cabling.

Most of the training in this field qualifies for college credit. You may be able to continue your education through various college programs and a variety of tuition assistance programs. Advanced training may also be available through classes offered by the armed forces.

Learn the Lingo

Here are a few words you'll hear in this career:

- **Bandwidth** A system's information-carrying capacity.
- **Network** Two or more computers linked together, either by wires or by wireless routers, so that they can share information.
- **Remote manageability** A term that describes the ability to administer a networked computer without physically touching the computer.

Finding a Job

Many young men and women enlist in the U.S. armed forces right out of high school. If you're 18 years old, you can simply sign up. At 17, you need a parent's permission.

To serve in the U.S. military, a person must pass physical requirements and a background check. Academically, an applicant must score at least a 31 on the Armed Forces

Qualification Test (AFQT). For the army, your service obligations would be determined at the recruiter's office. You can be signed up to serve from two to five years. In the Marine Corps, the initial time commitment is four to six years. (Read the fine print of your service contract carefully before you agree to sign anything to understand your possible length of service and number of tours.)

In the civilian world, people with good computer skills are in enormous demand. However, hardware and software change so quickly in this field that it is crucial to keep up with the latest innovations. This may require taking a few classes at the local technical college or getting an advanced degree. When working with computers, knowledge truly is power, and it keeps you marketable in the civilian world.

Find out about the job of information security specialist.

Tips for Success

- Good communications skills. You may have a tech job, but getting along with people remains a key component of your work. Grumpy or surly computer technicians, analysts, or managers rarely flourish in the field.

- Sometimes the customer is right! Just because you know more about computers doesn't mean you know more about the individual characteristics of particular systems you will be called upon to fix and maintain. Your colleagues' needs are what you are trying to meet.

Reality Check

As a computer systems specialist, you may spend many of your working hours communicating with people who have no idea what you're talking about. You have to be constantly willing to enlighten the less technically adept without getting frustrated or losing your temper.

Some Other Jobs to Think About

Computer operator or programmer, or systems administrator. Each military branch has a wide variety of subspecialties or other job classifications that include working with computers.

Engineering technician. Workers in engineering also use computers extensively. Engineering technicians use scientific knowledge to solve an endless series of practical problems in areas as diverse as industry, the environment, electronics, and aerospace.

Data entry. Want to work with computers without all that training? Data entry is an entry-level job for many people and often serves as a steppingstone to higher-paying jobs with increased responsibilities.

LEARN MORE ONLINE

CAREERS IN THE MILITARY
This Web site is the starting point for any investigation of jobs in the armed forces. It includes many useful job descriptions and links. http://www.careersinthemilitary.com

TODAY'S MILITARY
This site gives in-depth information on each branch of the U.S. armed forces. http://www.todaysmilitary.com

USENIX—THE ADVANCED COMPUTING SYSTEMS ASSOCIATION
Since 1975, the association—whose name comes from "Unix users group"—has brought together computer engineers, system administrators, scientists, and technicians working on the cutting edge of the computing world. http://www.usenix.org

ASSOCIATION FOR COMPUTING MACHINERY
The association delivers resources that advance computing as a science and a profession, and the Web site has a digital library as well as helpful publications, conferences, and career resources. http://www.acm.org

How to Move Up

- Advance in the military. In the armed services, promotions can come quickly, based on time in service and merit. After four years, you can become a senior computer systems specialist. In addition to handling other duties, these officers design and implement complex hardware and software programs for military organizations. They also test and debug computer systems. After 18 years, you can advance as high as computer systems operations supervisor. These officers manage entire computer centers.
- Advance in civilian life. Systems analysts can be promoted to senior or lead systems analyst. If you show you have leadership skills, you can become a project manager or advance into a management position. Specialized knowledge can be particularly useful if you plan on

working as an independent consultant or opening your own firm. Working with computers is very results driven; a successful career combines considerable experience with the most up-to-date knowledge.

TEXT-DEPENDENT QUESTIONS

1. ***What does the job of computer systems specialist entail?***
2. ***What is remote manageability?***
3. ***What are some related jobs you might consider?***

RESEARCH PROJECTS

1. ***Offer to help with network maintenance at your home, school, or other places. Learn as much as you can about the network and try to think of things that might make it work better. Pay attention to how you feel about the experience: Do you enjoy solving technical problems?***
2. ***Check out the free Web site Code Academy (https://www.codecademy.com/) and start learning how to write computer programs.***

Place Straps Over Arms

Medical Service Technician

Provide care during emergencies. Help prevent and treat diseases and injuries. Perform under life-and-death pressure.

4

WORDS TO UNDERSTAND

administrative: relating to the running of a business or organization.

ailment: an illness or injury.

harrowing: extremely upsetting.

post-traumatic stress disorder: a condition that develops after someone is exposed to severe trauma like in warfare.

Medical service technicians help keep the members of the U.S. armed forces fit for duty. They also provide medical care in critical situations. Physicians are not always immediately available to treat the injured or wounded during combat or other emergencies. In these cases, medical service technicians provide basic treatment and help care for sick and wounded service members. People's lives can depend on the quick reactions and effective care of medical service technicians. It is a career that offers the opportunity to help others.

◀ **A midshipman is strapped to a stretcher during damage control training aboard an aircraft carrier.**

Is This Job Right for You?

Would working as a medical service technician be a good fit for you? To find out, read each of the following questions and answer "Yes" or "No."

Yes **No** 1. *Are you motivated to help other people?*
Yes **No** 2. *Can you communicate effectively?*
Yes **No** 3. *Can you work under highly stressful conditions?*
Yes **No** 4. *Are you interested in the sciences?*
Yes **No** 5. *Are you detail-oriented?*
Yes **No** 6. *Are you willing to work in life-and-death situations?*
Yes **No** 7. *Are you patient?*
Yes **No** 8. *Are you sensitive to the needs of other people?*
Yes **No** 9. *Are you willing to take care of someone else's physical needs?*
Yes **No** 10. *Do you have a friendly manner?*

If you answered "Yes" to most of these questions, you might consider a career as a medical service technician. To find out more about this job, read on.

What's the Work Like?

As a medical service technician, you would keep service members healthy and return them to health if they become sick or injured. Sometimes, these two roles involve the same procedures. The job entails both routine and emergency medical duties.

On the routine side, medical service technicians help examine and treat patients who have minor injuries or common diseases. You would take the patient's temperature, pulse, and blood pressure, as well as collect blood samples, record

TALKING MONEY

Personnel with one to four years of service in the armed forces earn from $19,000 to $25,000 per year in base salary. Benefits—including health care, tuition support, career training, and life insurance—are excellent, and active-duty service people receive many other benefits, as well. People with previous medical experience may qualify for signing bonuses and/or higher salaries. In civilian life, an emergency medical technician (EMT) is a comparable job to a medical service technician. According to 2016 data from the U.S. Bureau of Labor Statistics, the annual mean salary for EMTs is $32,670.

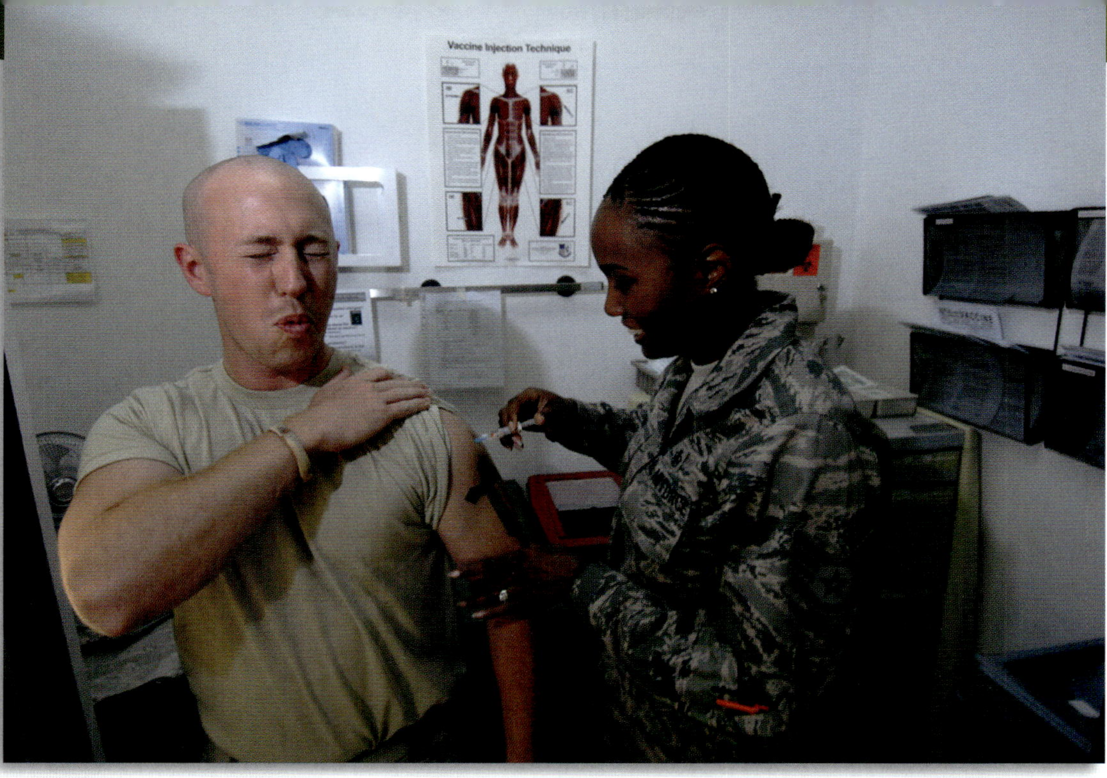

▲ **A soldier receives a hepatitis B vaccine.**

test results, operate X-ray equipment, and change bandages and dressings. Technicians also prepare operating rooms, equipment, and supplies for surgery and perform some preoperative and postoperative care. You may also give shots and medicines to patients.

The job also has an **administrative** component. It is the medical service technician's job to interview patients, record their medical histories, and maintain treatment records. You might also be assigned to keep health records and clinical files up to date.

During wartime, you would assist physicians and dentists with emergency medical treatment. Injured or wounded service members need immediate treatment. When physicians are not readily available, you would be authorized to step in to provide basic medical or dental treatment to battlefield casualties. In this role, you would perform medical procedures, suture wounds, and apply casts to broken limbs. In special circumstances, you might even administer substances such as nitroglycerin, glucose, epinephrine, and albuterol. In the field, a medical service technician is a sort of jack-of-all-trades of medical care.

Medics sometimes accompany patrols to care for injuries if necessary. In such situations, you would be wearing body armor and a helmet and carrying your weapons at all times. This can be scary because attacks can come at any time. Wartime injuries can be particularly bloody and traumatic compared with the typical emergencies in the United States. As a medical service technician, you would need to prepare to help fellow recruits under possibly **harrowing** conditions.

Who's Hiring?

- All branches of the military. (The U.S. Navy handles medical services for the Marine Corps.)
- Medcom. The U.S. Army Medical Command, headquartered in San Antonio, Texas. In addition to providing medical care to a large patient population, it also conducts training, and plans and maintains readiness for wartime health care operations.
- A military hospital. For example, Walter Reed Army Medical Center, in Washington, D.C., has a staff of over 7,000 people, providing care to active and retired personnel from all branches of the military.

Where Are the Jobs?

Medical service technicians usually work in hospitals and clinics. These might be in combat zones, at military bases, or aboard ships or submarines. The job requires a great deal of bending, kneeling, and heavy lifting. Pulled muscles are a common **ailment**. The condition known as **post-traumatic stress disorder** (PTSD) is also a possibility for people new to working in health care. Many medical service technicians have prior experience working with gunshot wounds and car wrecks, but even they sometimes have trouble coping with the random violence.

Medical service technicians may give emergency medical treatment in the field. In a combat area, such as in Iraq or Afghanistan, you may find yourself accompanying patrols or helping in transporting

TALKING TRENDS

As long as people need medical and dental services, medical service technicians will be in demand. The military offers an opportunity for high school graduates to get training and experience in the medical and dental professions. In civilian life, emergency medical technicians and paramedics held about 241,000 jobs in 2014. That number is expected to grow considerably over the next 10 years, according to the Bureau of Labor Statistics.

the wounded in dangerous situations. Medical service technicians deal with the same sorts of situations that EMTs do in the United States except that, in the field, they may see a lot more physical trauma. In a battlefield situation, for instance, you may have to treat abdominal, head, and chest wounds.

Sometimes medical technicians work standard hours assisting with outpatient and inpatient care and treatment. However, emergency services function 24 hours a day, and hospitals can't close for Christmas or the Fourth of July. This means you may have to work irregular working hours.

A Typical Day

Here are some highlights for a typical day as a medical service technician.

Vaccinate service members. This morning, you will help to vaccinate recruits against measles, mumps, and rubella (MMR), regardless of their prior history. You'll help organize the flow of work, assist the administering physician and nurse, and perhaps help give the shots.

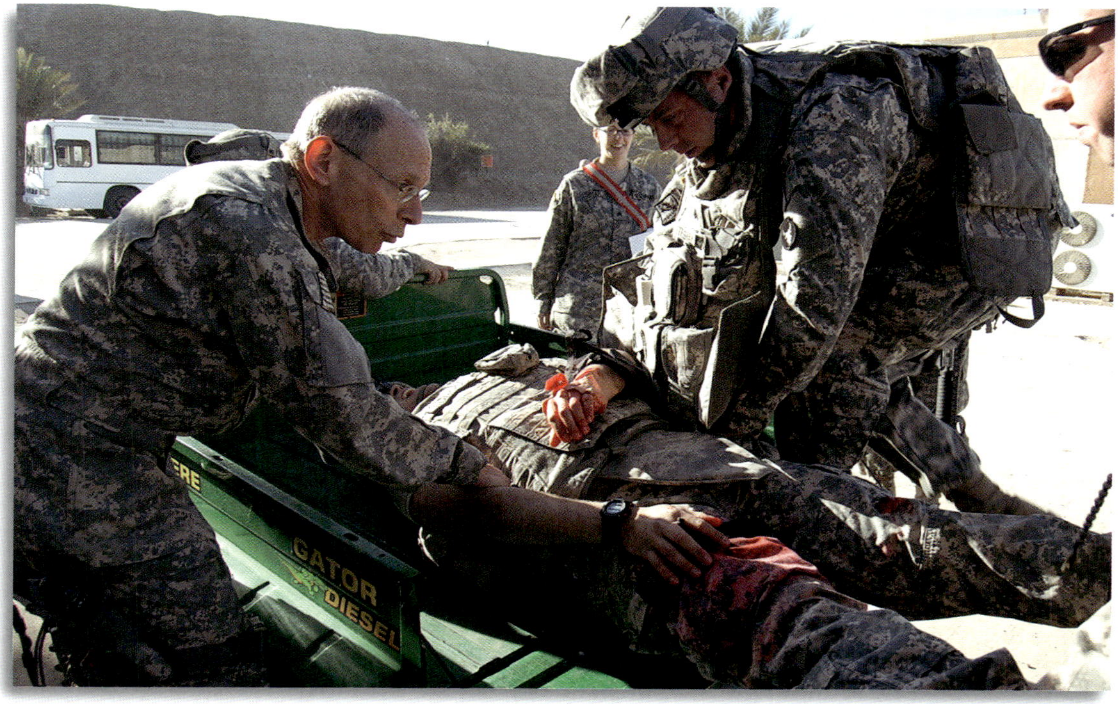

▲ Soldiers take part in mass casualty training to learn how to handle a medical emergency.

Prepare the operating room for surgery. You'll make sure there are sufficient operating rooms, equipment, and supplies for all surgeries scheduled in the afternoon. If supplies are low, you'll order them.

See what it's like to be an army medic.

Provide emergency medical care. A solider has choked on a chicken bone at dinner. You look for ABC: airway, breathing, and circulation. He's not breathing, so you do intubation (place a tube down the throat and into the windpipe). There's no pulse, so you do cardiopulmonary resuscitation (CPR). The soldier is alive, but full recovery is uncertain. Accidents happen every day in a population as large as that of the armed services.

Start Preparing Now

- Take relevant high school classes. Good subject choices include chemistry, biology, psychology, math, and general science.
- Become a first responder. This is an excellent way to acquire experience. Requirements for first responders vary from state to state. In general, it takes about 40 hours of training over about two months. If you cannot do this, at least volunteer at a hospital or trauma center.

Training and How to Get It

Job training for a medical service technician in the armed forces consists of about nine weeks of basic training. This is followed by as few as seven or as many as 52 weeks of advanced training in the classroom and in the field. The amount of training depends on your specialty.

In classes, you will study the human body and biology in some detail and then learn basic nursing care. Your instructors will also cover wide-ranging topics such as surgical and laboratory procedures, diagnosing diseases, sterilizing surgical equipment, and plaster-casting techniques.

Medical service technicians play an important part in medical care on the battlefield. Because of this, some of your training will focus on recognizing and treating life-threatening emergencies outside the hospital environment. You'll receive instruction and practice in dealing with medical emergencies such as bleeding, fractures, cardiac arrest, seizures, and airway

NOTES FROM THE FIELD

***Chief petty officer,** Naval Training Station, Great Lakes, Illinois*

Q: ***How did you get your job?***

A: **I always knew that I wanted to go into the medical profession. My mom has been ill throughout my life, so I spent a lot of time in hospitals while I was growing up. Plus, I like taking care of people. After navy boot camp, I trained to become a hospital corpsman. Then, I received specialized training at the Field Medical Service School (FMSS) in Camp LeJeune, North Carolina, to learn how to handle field and trauma medicine with marines.**

Q: ***What do you like best about your job?***

A: **I have had many great experiences. Recently, I was stationed for several months in Umm Qasr, a port in southern Iraq. There, I was . . . training the Iraqi navy and marines on various medical platforms, and I oversaw the building and staffing of a medical clinic.**

Q: ***What's the most challenging part of your job?***

A: **Once trained, you are responsible for the treatment of every medical condition imaginable—from arm fractures to appendicitis to heart attacks. So, when I was deployed on a fast-attack nuclear-powered submarine, I had to make sure that the sailors were healthy, both physically and mentally, especially because submarines can be at sea for long periods at a time. I gave immunizations, counseled the sailors, and monitored the radiation levels of all personnel on board due to their exposure to nuclear power.**

Q: ***What are the keys to success to being a medical service technician?***

A: **[Providing] the best possible care to new recruits.**

obstruction. You'll also learn how to manage serious injuries such as falls, fractures, cuts, and burns. All this training also requires you to know how to use emergency equipment such as backboards, suction devices, splints, oxygen delivery systems, and stretchers. Medical service technicians must also be proficient in CPR.

▲ **Army medics take part in a medical training exercise.**

Further medical training occurs as you gain experience in your position. You can also take advanced courses. Some technicians may specialize in fields such as radiology, search and rescue, and preventive medicine

Most of your training in the medical and dental fields can be applied for credit at colleges and universities. With study and experience, you may qualify for certification with the National Registry of Emergency Medical Technicians (NREMT), a terrific résumé-builder that shows you have mastered the techniques of basic care.

Learn the Lingo

Here are a few words you'll hear in this career:

- **Debridement** The cleaning of an open wound by removing dead tissue and foreign material. Debridement of burns is extremely painful.
- **Myocardial infarction** A heart attack.
- **Sepsis** A very severe infection.
- **Thrombosis** A blood clot.
- **Venipuncture** The drawing of blood from a vein.

Finding a Job

Many young men and women enlist in the armed forces right out of high school. Eighteen-year-olds can do so on their own; 17-year-olds can enlist with a parent's permission.

To serve in the U.S. military, a person must pass physical requirements and a background check. Academically, an applicant must score at least a 31 on the Armed Forces Qualification Test (AFQT). For the army, your service obligations would be determined at the recruiter's office. You can agree with the recruiter to serve for two, three, four, or even five years.

In civilian life, private ambulance services or hospitals advertise medical service jobs on the Internet and in newspapers. Job openings are sometimes posted by local governments for work in fire departments, public ambulance services, and emergency medical services.

LEARN MORE ONLINE

CAREERS IN THE MILITARY

This Web site is the starting point for any investigation of jobs in the armed forces. It includes many useful job descriptions and links. http://www.careersinthemilitary.com

TODAY'S MILITARY

This site gives in-depth information on each branch of the U.S. armed forces. http://www.todaysmilitary.com

NATIONAL ASSOCIATION OF EMERGENCY MEDICAL TECHNICIANS (NAEMT)

The NAEMT, founded in 1975, is the nation's largest and oldest organization representing EMTs and paramedics. This Web site has information about educational programs and research and many useful links. http://www.naemt.org

Tips for Success

- Keep calm and be personable. Even routine medical care will make some patients nervous. Your job will be much easier if you remain calm and friendly.
- Learn from those around you. The practical lessons of doing medical work under sometimes-stressful circumstances will be many. If you steadily build on and improve your techniques, you may go far in the field of medicine.

Reality Check

This job is not for the faint of heart or the easily depressed. There can be a lot of blood and gore, and the work is physically strenuous. In addition, dealing with life-or-death situations and suffering or dying patients can be extremely stressful.

Some Other Jobs to Think About

Military possibilities. In the armed forces, other comparable careers include operating room specialist, preventive medicine specialist, radiology specialist, and respiratory specialist. These jobs all require quick and level-headed reactions to life-or-death situations.

Civilian possibilities. Emergency medical technicians treat victims of accidents, fire, or heart attacks. Medical assistants work for physicians and perform routine medical and clerical tasks. Medication aides give shots and medicine under the supervision of physicians. Physician assistants perform routine examinations and treatment for physicians.

▲ **Commissioned Officer Training School students take part in a simulated deployment scenario exercise. The exercise tests their decision-making skills as well as their contingency operations knowledge.**

How to Move Up

- Advance in the military. In the armed forces promotions can come quickly, based on time in service and merit. After several years, medical service technicians can advance into supervisory positions. After 18 years, you can advance as high as medical services coordinator. These officers oversee training, health care, and disaster control programs.

- Advance in civilian life. In civilian life, emergency medical training is offered at progressive levels: EMT-1 (basic), EMT-2 (intermediate), EMT-3, and EMT-4 (paramedic). To advance in this career requires progressively harder coursework as well as clinical and field experience. Advancement beyond the paramedic level usually means leaving fieldwork completely to become a supervisor, operations manager, or executive director of emergency services. If you like the health care field, you can return to school and become a registered nurse, physician, or other health care worker.

TEXT-DEPENDENT QUESTIONS

1. ***What procedures might a medical service technician perform?***
2. ***What is Medcom?***
3. ***What is the NAEMT and what does it do?***
4. ***What are the levels of civilian emergency medical training?***

RESEARCH PROJECTS

1. ***Get started on this career now by taking a first-aid course such as those offered by the Red Cross (http://www.redcross.org/m/phssmrd/take-a-class). Your school, local community college, or firehouse might also offer classes.***
2. ***To get a better sense of what this job is like, there are many memoirs you can read, such as:*** **Lest We Forget: An Army Ranger Medic's Story** ***by Leo Jenkins;*** **On Call in Hell: One Doctor's Iraq War Story** ***by Cdr. Richard Jadick; and*** **Not on My Watch: The 21st Century Combat Medic** ***by Joshua R. Fansler and Joshua M. Peters.***

Machinist

5

Craft machine parts by hand. Keep equipment running. Solve mechanical problems.

WORDS TO UNDERSTAND

lathe: a machine for shaping metal or wood.
lubricate: to apply a substance (for example, oil) to reduce friction.
precision: something highly exact.
ventilated: having good air circulation.

Engines and machines can break down no matter how well they are maintained. The engines and machines of the U.S. armed forces are not any different. If the machines are expensive, someone has to repair broken parts, and sometimes, those parts are not available. In these cases, new parts must be made. This is the machinist's job. They perform incredibly accurate work—sometimes to within a margin of 1/10,000th of an inch—and so require amazing concentration and physical effort. Without the intelligence and hard work of machinists, the high-tech equipment of the U.S. armed forces would turn into nothing more than a bunch of metal surrounded by wires.

◀ **A machinist will learn to use lots of heavy equipment. Here a torch cutter burns through tough metal.**

Is This Job Right for You?

Would working as a machinist be a good fit for you? To find out, read each of the following questions and answer "Yes" or "No."

Yes **No** 1. *Do you enjoy solving mechanical problems?*
Yes **No** 2. *Are you extremely detail-oriented?*
Yes **No** 3. *Do you like to work with your hands?*
Yes **No** 4. *Do you like to apply mathematical formulas?*
Yes **No** 5. *Can you concentrate in a noisy environment?*
Yes **No** 6. *Do you enjoy making things?*
Yes **No** 7. *Can you work independently?*
Yes **No** 8. *Do you like a job that requires physical effort?*
Yes **No** 9. *Do you enjoy a challenge?*
Yes **No** 10. *Are you willing to work standing up most of the day?*

If you answered "Yes" to most of these questions, you might consider a career as a machinist. To find out more about this job, read on.

What's the Work Like?

As a machinist in the armed forces, you would make, repair, and modify metal and non-metal parts for engines and other types of machines. You'd operate tools such as **lathes**, drill presses, grinders, shapers, hacksaws, band saws, and milling machines. You might be taught how to use all these machines or you might specialize in one or two. You'd then use your skill with machine tools to plan and make machined products that meet exact specifications.

The nature of the machinist's job is changing quickly. Many machinists today now use tools that are "computer numerically controlled," also known as CNC. In this case, you'd work with computer control programmers to decide how the automated equipment will cut a part. The programmer may

TALKING MONEY

Salaries in the U.S. armed forces depend on performance and time in service. In general, a machinist with three years of experience makes about $2,500 a month, in addition to excellent benefits. In civilian life, according to 2016 data from the U.S. Bureau of Labor Statistics, machinists average about $43,000 per year.

▲ **An aviation machinist and an aviation machinist's mate align a propeller on a P-3C Orion.**

choose the path of the cut while you would determine the type and speed of the cutting tool and the feed rate. Most machinists now train in CNC programming. They may write basic programs and then change the programs based on problems in test runs. Machinists may also operate the CNC machines themselves after the production process is designed.

Some **precision** machinists produce small batches or one-of-a-kind items. Others, known as production machinists, produce large quantities of one specific part. This process is almost completely automated, and the machine tools operate without anyone present. One production machinist, working an eight-hour day, might check equipment, replace worn cutting tools, and perform other tasks on several CNC machines that operate 24 hours a day.

After the work is completed, machinists check the accuracy of their work against blueprints. They use tools such as micrometers, calipers, rulers, and depth gauges.

Modern production techniques require machinists to have a wide range of skills. Constantly working with million-dollar machinery and equipment carries a great deal of pressure. However, if you are technically oriented, have strong troubleshooting skills, and enjoy working with your hands, you might love the challenges of working as a machinist.

▲ A machinist's mate checks the pressure of a liquid oxygen cart.

Who's Hiring?

- Army
- Navy
- Air force
- Marine corps
- Coast guard

Where Are the Jobs?

As a machinist in the military, you would enjoy better-than-average working conditions for this profession. Most machine shops in the U.S. armed

TALKING TRENDS

Machinists will always be needed because anything with gears, electronics, or wiring eventually breaks down. In civilian life, machinists hold about 477,000 jobs. The Bureau of Labor Statistics projects that the employment of machinists will grow at about 10 percent, or more quickly than the average for other occupations through at least 2024.

forces are relatively clean, well lit, and **ventilated**. Machine shops can be noisy places, but many computer-controlled machines in military shops are partially or completely enclosed. This reduces the exposure of machinists to noise, dirt, and the lubricants used to cool workpieces during machining.

However, the job still requires stamina. Machinists stand most of the day and occasionally need to lift heavy workpieces. Many military machine shops try to reduce the problem of heavy lifting using autoloaders and overhead cranes. Most machinists work a 40-hour week. However, you may occasionally have to work evening and weekend shifts if the demand is urgent.

In civilian life, most machinists work in small machine shops or in manufacturing industries, such as machinery manufacturing and transportation equipment manufacturing (for cars and planes). Maintenance machinists work in almost all industries that use any kind of production machinery.

See what goes on at a military machine shop.

▲ A U.S. Navy aviation machinist mate helps replace the engine of a Seahawk helicopter in the hangar bay of an aircraft carrier in the South China Sea.

A Typical Day

Here are some highlights for a typical day as an armed forces machinist.

Review the blueprints. Before you "machine" a part, you carefully plan and prepare the operation. Your job is to repair a broken part, so you study the electronic and written blueprints. You also examine the specifications for the job.

Make the calculations. You calculate where to cut or bore into the workpiece and how fast to feed it into the machine. Then you choose the proper tools and materials for the job and finishing operations.

Machine the workpiece. Finally, the prep work is completed. You position the workpiece on the machine tool, set the controls, and make the cuts. You constantly check the feed rate and speed of the machine and make sure the workpiece is being properly **lubricated** and cooled. The temperature of the workpiece is very important because most metals expand when heated. Machinists must consider temperature and adjust the size of their cuts.

Start Preparing Now

- Take relevant classes in high school. Helpful school subjects include mathematics (especially trigonometry), general science, metalworking, blueprint reading, drafting, and/or mechanical drawing.
- Get some experience. Any practical experience with machine tools would be extremely valuable. If possible, try to find an apprenticeship program for machine setters, operators, or tenders.
- Take a vocational course. Many machinists learn the trade through two-year associate's degree programs at community or technical colleges. Try a course in mechanics, machine shop, electricity, or practical math.

Training and How to Get It

Job training for a military machinist usually begins with nine weeks of basic training, in which you'll learn basic soldiering skills. This will be followed by about 14 weeks of advanced individual training, including practice in machine operation. Part of this time

NOTES FROM THE FIELD

***Staff sergeant,** Aberdeen Proving Ground, Aberdeen, Maryland*

Q: ***How did you get your job as a machinist?***

A: **I joined the Army Reserves for training so I could do something different from my civilian job as a clerk. . . . For a year, I worked several weekends a month with my reserve unit; then I volunteered for active duty, and I asked to receive training as a machinist. I thought the work would be challenging and different and would allow me to prove myself. I went through initial training [and] I learned the basic skills required of all machinists. I was able to learn my trade quickly and became familiar with some of the other occupations in the maintenance shop. . . . I [have also] supervised a crew that repaired jeeps, tanks, and other armored equipment.**

Q: ***What do you like best about your job?***

A: **[I like] helping to make repairs to everything from radios to helicopters.**

Q: ***What is the most challenging part of your job?***

A: **I was recently promoted to staff sergeant and look forward to being one of the top-ranking females in the maintenance field. I like the challenge of being the only female in the unit.**

Q: ***What are the keys to success to being a machinist?***

A: **[Continue to] learn the latest technologies. And just have fun.**

is spent in the classroom and part in on-the-job training. Classroom instruction includes math, physics, science, blueprint reading, mechanical drawing, quality control, and safety practices. Some other skills you'll learn include recognizing machine types; mastering their uses, setup, and operation; and learning the various qualities of different metals. In field training, an experienced machinist supervises apprentices while they learn how to operate various machine tools. The length and nature of your training depend on your job.

▲ **A machinist mate uses a needle gun on a watertight hatch.**

As machine shops have increased their use of computer-controlled equipment, training in the operation and programming of CNC machine tools has become essential. Engineers keep creating new types of machine tools and new materials to machine, so machinists must constantly receive extra training to update their skills. The military may provide this training, or a representative of the equipment manufacturer may provide it. In addition to operating machines that use metal cutting tools, machinists sometimes use machines that cut with lasers, water jets, or electrified wires. Though some of the computer controls may be similar, machinists must understand the unique cutting properties of these different machines.

Further training occurs on the job and through advanced courses. Some machinist's jobs offer accelerated promotions to higher pay grades. The training you would receive as a machinist may count as credit hours toward a bachelor's or associate's degree. You may also receive an opportunity for continued education through various armed forces college programs in addition to tuition assistance.

Learn the Lingo

Here are a few words you'll hear in this career:

- **CNC machines** Abbreviation for "computer numerically controlled" machines. CNC machines follow a computer program that can control the cutting tool speed, change dull tools, and perform all of the necessary cuts to create a part.
- **Machine tool** A drill press, lathe, grinder, milling machine, or other type of machine, usually used to work metal.
- **Workpiece** The piece of steel, aluminum, titanium, plastic, silicon, or any other material that is being shaped.

Finding a Job

Many young men and women enlist in the armed forces right out of high school. At 18 years old, you can enlist on your own; 17-year-olds need the permission of a parent.

To serve in the U.S. military, a person must pass physical requirements and a background check. Academically, an applicant must score at least a 31 on the Armed Forces Qualification Test (AFQT). For the army, your service obligations would be determined at the recruiter's office. You can agree with the recruiter to serve for two, three, four, or even five years. (Read the fine print of your service contract carefully before you agree to sign anything to understand your possible length of service and number of tours of duty.)

Tips for Success

- Good machinists work with their heads as much as their hands. An ability to read blueprints and apply mathematical formulas is indispensable. Most machinists now rely on computer-aided design (CAD) programs, so good computer skills are also crucial.
- The old adage from carpentry is also appropriate in the work of a machinist: Measure twice, cut once. Pausing to check one's work is always a good idea.

Reality Check

Machinists may work far from battlefields, but this does not mean the job has no risks. Workers around machine tools need to wear protective equipment, such as safety glasses, to shield against bits of flying metal. They also spend many days using earplugs to dampen machinery noise. Handling hazardous coolants and lubricants requires caution. It's safer than being in the infantry, but not as safe a job as a finance and accounting specialist, for example.

Some Other Jobs to Think About

Tool and die maker. These highly skilled machinists produce tools, dies, and parts of machines used to manufacture a variety of products.

Welder. This job also requires precision and skill in working with metal.

Auto or truck mechanic. There's always a shortage of good transportation mechanics, especially as car engines become increasingly complex.

LEARN MORE ONLINE

CAREERS IN THE MILITARY

This Web site is the starting point for any investigation of jobs in the armed forces. It includes many useful job descriptions and links. http://www.careersinthemilitary.com

TODAY'S MILITARY

This site gives in-depth information on each branch of the U.S. armed forces. http://www.todaysmilitary.com

PRECISION METALFORMING ASSOCIATION (PMA)

The PMA Educational Foundation, established in 1996, is a good source for training information for this field. http://www.pma.org

INTERNATIONAL ASSOCIATION OF MACHINISTS AND AEROSPACE WORKERS

The largest machinist's union contains a great deal of information of interest to anyone beginning this career. http://www.goiam.org

How to Move Up

- Advance in the military. In the armed forces, promotions can come quickly, based on time in service and merit. After three years, you will become eligible to be a senior machinist. Among other duties, senior machinists perform difficult machine setup and operation for precision work. After 16 years, you can advance as high as a mechanical maintenance superintendent. These officers oversee all shop administration at a facility.

- Advance in civilian life. Civilian factories and repair shops in many industries, such as the electrical product, automotive, and heavy machinery industries, are always looking for experienced machinists. Experienced machinists may become CNC programmers or tool and die makers. It is also possible to be promoted to a supervisory position in a firm. Promotions usually depend on experience, job evaluations, and extra classroom training.

TEXT-DEPENDENT QUESTIONS

1. *What is the difference between a precision and a production machinist?*
2. *What are CNC machines?*
3. *What are some of the possible risks of this profession?*

RESEARCH PROJECTS

1. *You don't need a high-tech machine shop to start learning this trade; lots of people are interested in machinery as a hobby. Check out the Hobby Machinist (www.hobby-machinist.com) or Home Shop Machinist (http://www.homeshopmachinist.net/) to see how you can get started.*
2. *If you look online, there are probably multiple machine shops within driving distance of where you live. Find one, get in touch with them, and ask if someone at the company would talk to you about how they do what they do. You might be able to get a tour of the facility, so you can get a sense of what it feels like to work in that environment.*

Law Enforcement and Security Specialist

6

Hold a position of respect and authority. Investigate crimes. Protect lives and property.

WORDS TO UNDERSTAND

apprehension: the act of being caught or arrested.
espionage: spying.
maritime: relating to the ocean.

An officer fudges the books to steal money. Two soldiers get into a brutal fight over whose hometown team is better. Crimes occur in all large organizations; the U.S. military is no exception. Law enforcement and security specialists are the military's police officers. They investigate crimes committed on military property or those that involve service members of the U.S. armed forces.

Law enforcement and security specialists are also the armed forces' first line of defense. It is their job to maintain discipline on all military bases and installations. Military police protect lives and property by enforcing military rules and regulations. This is a career for you if you want to investigate accidents and crimes, prepare reports on the incidents, and arrest suspects when necessary.

◀ **An airman from the Security Police Group stands guard near an aircraft during Operation Desert Shield.**

Is This Job Right for You?

Would working as a law enforcement and security specialist be a good fit for you? To find out, read each of the following questions and answer "Yes" or "No."

Yes *No* **1.** *Can you work well independently and as a member of a team?*
Yes *No* **2.** *Are you sensitive to others' feelings and needs?*
Yes *No* **3.** *Are you willing to perform potentially dangerous work?*
Yes *No* **4.** *Are you willing to work outdoors most of the day?*
Yes *No* **5.** *Can you learn and apply rules, regulations, and laws?*
Yes *No* **6.** *Do you believe in the importance of the law?*
Yes *No* **7.** *Do you enjoy working with people?*
Yes *No* **8.** *Are you honest, reliable, and responsible?*
Yes *No* **9.** *Can you remain alert and calm in stressful situations?*
Yes *No* **10.** *Can you think and react quickly?*

If you answered "Yes" to most of these questions, you might consider a career as a law enforcement and security officer. To find out more about this job, read on.

What's the Work Like?

The work of law enforcement and security specialists is often similar to the work of a civilian police officer. You would control traffic, prevent crime, and respond to emergencies. You'd patrol an assigned area on foot, by car, or by boat to prevent crimes and enforce military rules and regulations. To do this, you may search people, vehicles, property, and places. You may have to pursue suspects, control those who resist **apprehension**, and even use firearms and other weapons. All of these tasks require you to retain your self-control in potentially explosive situations.

However, you would also have military-specific duties. Law enforcement specialists guard the entrances to military bases and direct the

TALKING MONEY

Military jobs pay according to seniority, and for the first two years, the base annual salaries do not rise very far above $19,000. Benefits include tuition support and health and life insurance. The median annual salary for civilian police officers is over $60,000, according to 2016 data from the U.S. Bureau of Labor Statistics.

movement of people and traffic. You might have to guard inmates in military correctional facilities. When the United States invaded Iraq in 2003, many law enforcement specialists were used to control the large numbers of detainees being held by U.S. forces. Military police were also assigned to conduct raids and participate in regular patrols.

Another military-specific duty would be to investigate criminal activities and activities related to **espionage**, treason, and terrorism. This might involve interviewing witnesses, victims, and suspects; collecting fingerprints and other evidence; and arresting criminal suspects. You might have to testify or present evidence in a military court proceeding.

The U.S. Coast Guard and the U.S. Navy share responsibility for protecting important ports—both overseas and in the United States—against the threat of terrorism and other acts of **maritime** crime.

▲ **Personnel from the U.S. Coast Guard Law Enforcement confiscate an estimated $78 million worth of cocaine.**

Who's Hiring?

- All five branches need service members who maintain discipline and enforce the law.
- A variety of subdivisions. The Military Police Corps serves as the law enforcement arm of the U.S. Army, while the U.S. Marine Corps version is known as the Provost Marshal's Office. In the navy, law enforcement personnel are assigned to the Master-at-Arms branch. The Air Force Security Forces police the U.S. Air Force.

Where Are the Jobs?

Law enforcement and security specialists in the military might work indoors or outdoors depending on their assignment. Some have desk jobs and work in air-conditioned comfort. Others conduct investigations or patrol facilities and are at the mercy of the weather. Law enforcement and security specialists, like police officers, face dangerous and unpredictable situations. They must go anywhere a crime is committed, regardless of location, time of day, and climate.

The navy's law force is deployed to many spots worldwide, including Iraq, Afghanistan, and southern Africa. They may be assigned to a mobile security force detachment, performing missions that involve boarding ships with minimal defense capability, fortifying landside locations, and securing foreign ports for use by U.S. warships.

In civilian life, positions such as a police officer can be found throughout the United States. In 2017, police officers held more than 800,000 jobs.

A Typical Day

Here are some highlights for a typical day as a law enforcement and security specialist in a combat zone.

Clear a supply route. You might be ordered to monitor a major supply route in Iraq. You'll be briefed at 6:30 a.m. and then drive the route to the checkpoint. You'll look for hostile activity, enemy personnel, or anything that looks out of place from previous runs.

Report trouble. Once you travel the route and are sure

See a day in the life of a military police officer.

▲ As a law enforcement and security specialist, you may work in a variety of places. You could work on a boat or you could work to secure trains in the big cities. There are many opportunities in this line of work.

it is clear, you'll radio back to the convoy commanders and let them know it's safe. If you find something suspicious, you will radio back to headquarters, and traffic on the route will be stopped.

Look for trouble. After the convoy is clear, you might stop along the route and wait for trouble. This might include improvised explosive devices (IEDs), small arms fire, or vehicle breakdowns.

TALKING TRENDS

Fear of terrorism has increased the demand for military police services. For example, the number of navy law enforcement specialists has expanded from about 3,500 to more than 10,000. This is due to their expanding role in antiterrorism protection duties, rather than in law enforcement. Civilian police officers are expected to grow at an average rate overall, but much depends on crime rates in particular areas.

Start Preparing Now

- Work at the mall. Even a part-time security job at the mall will give you a feel for this kind of work. It will also look good when it comes time to choose a career specialty in the military.
- Take some college-level classes. People with some training in police science, criminal justice, or law enforcement have a huge edge in receiving their career choice. Any prior experience in law enforcement or military experience with combat skills is extremely valuable.
- Make sure you are physically fit. Many law enforcement positions require strength, stamina, and agility.

Training and How to Get It

Job training for a law enforcement and security specialists in the armed forces usually consists of about nine weeks of basic training followed by 8 to 12 weeks of individual training and on-the-job instruction. Training length varies depending on specialty.

Law enforcement training includes instruction in military rules and regulations. You will also receive training in the use of firearms, self-defense, first aid, and emergency response. Instructors also teach prisoner control and discipline, investigation and evidence collection procedures, communication skills, traffic and crowd control techniques, and the use of different types of law enforcement equipment. Your training will also probably include on-the-job experience with a veteran officer.

Some branches have training that is more specific. For the U.S. Air Force, security forces students attend the Air Force Security Forces Academy at Lackland Air Force Base in Texas, where they complete a lengthy course that teaches basic military police functions, including missile security, convoy actions, capture and recovery of nuclear weapons, law enforcement, and directing traffic. The course also teaches nonlethal tactics, such as using pepper spray and pressure points on a body to subdue people.

In the military, you may be able to receive specialized training in a single type of security work, such as chemical analysis, firearms instruction, or handwriting and fingerprint identification. For example, at the U.S. Army Military Police School, you can take courses in areas such as crisis/hostage negotiations, military working-dog handling, and weapons of mass destruction crime scene processing.

▲ **Training to be a law enforcement specialist can be physically exhausting, but these training sessions will ensure that the specialists are the best in their field.**

NOTES FROM THE FIELD

Provost sergeant, *Marine Corps Headquarters, Washington, D.C.*

Q: ***How did you get your job?***

A: **After completing one year of study in criminal justice at Northeastern University in Boston, I began looking for a different kind of challenge. I felt as though I was doing many of the same things I had done in high school. Seeking a way to prove myself, I enlisted in the Marine Corps as a military police officer (MP) at Camp Pendleton, where I performed base security duties.**

Q: ***What do you like best about your job?***

A: **I like the training and travel. I had the opportunity to attend the Federal Bureau of Investigation (FBI) National Academy. . . . This enabled me to advance further in the criminal investigation arena. As an investigator, I gathered crime evidence, interrogated suspects, and interviewed witnesses. . . . I also had the opportunity to travel to Hawaii, Japan, and other locations.**

Q: ***What's the most challenging part of your job?***

A: **The role of a patrol officer enforcing laws within the base community [has been most challenging for me]. In this position, I responded to emergency situations, such as robberies, assaults, and accidents.**

Q: ***What are the keys to success for your job?***

A: **[One key was receiving] extensive investigative training . . . at the FBI National Academy.**

Learn the Lingo

Here are a few words you'll hear in this career:

- **AWOL** U.S. military personnel become AWOL (absent without official leave) when they are absent from their post without a valid pass or leave. The Marine Corps and navy usually refer to this as UA, or "unauthorized absence." Law enforcement personnel have to find these people, often known as deserters.

- **Master-at-Arms** In the U.S. Navy, master-at-arms is the specialty concerned with law enforcement and police work.

- **MP** This is the acronym for "military police," the law enforcement branch of the U.S. Army.

- **MSST** MSSTs (maritime safety and security teams) are organized by the U.S. Coast Guard. They can be deployed anywhere in the country to provide increased security on the water or the shore.

- **10-24** Military police code for a suspicious person.

Finding a Job

Many young men and women enlist in the armed forces right out of high school. An 18-year-old high school graduate can walk into the local recruiter's office and enlist. Seventeen-year-olds can also enlist but need a parent's permission.

To serve in the U.S. military, a person must pass physical requirements and a background check. For the army, service obligations are determined at the recruiter's office. You can agree with the recruiter to serve for two, three, four, or even five years. In the Marine Corps, the initial time commitment is usually four to six years. (Read the fine print of your service contract carefully before you agree to sign anything to understand your potential length of service and number of tours of duty.)

In civilian life, most police departments require at least a high school diploma. Police positions are also controlled by civil service regulations, so you will have to take a written examination and then be interviewed by senior officers. You will also take a physical exam, which typically include tests of vision, hearing, strength, and agility. You can get additional information about becoming a police officer from local, state, and federal law enforcement agencies.

Tips for Success

- Develop good judgment. Military police work requires good judgment and faultless ethical behavior in all situations.

- Have quick reactions. One of the keys to the job is to maintain alertness in extreme conditions, particularly when preceded by long periods of boredom or relatively low stress.

LEARN MORE ONLINE

CAREERS IN THE MILITARY
This Web site is the starting point for any investigation of jobs in the armed forces. It includes many useful job descriptions and links. http://www.careersinthemilitary.com

TODAY'S MILITARY
This site gives in-depth information on each branch of the U.S. armed forces. http://www.todaysmilitary.com

U.S. ARMY MILITARY POLICE SCHOOL
This is the official site and contains specific information as well as useful links. http://www.wood.army.mil/usamps

Reality Check

Police work, whether military or civilian, can be stressful and dangerous. Police officers always need to be ready to deal with threatening situations. Law enforcement officers often witness the death and suffering that result from accidents and crimes. A career in law enforcement can put some individuals at risk of depression.

Some Other Jobs to Think About

Correctional officer. A correctional officer guards and supervises inmates in a prison or jail. It's a law enforcement job with more routine work.

Security guard. Security guards are sometimes confused with the police because of similar uniforms and responsibilities. However, a security guard's power comes from a private contract, not from the government.

Private detective or investigator. These jobs are similar to police work. They involve collecting evidence and conducting investigations and surveillance.

How to Move Up

- Advance in the military. In the armed forces, promotions are awarded based on time in service and merit. After four years, you can achieve a supervisory job, such as a squad leader. After 18 years, you can rise to the level of law enforcement superintendent. These officers manage security forces on larger bases.

- Advance in civilian life. Civilian law enforcement and security specialists work for state, county, or city law enforcement agencies. They may also work in prisons, intelligence agencies, and private security companies. In most civilian police departments, promotions to detective, corporal, and higher positions are usually based on a combination of your score on a written examination and your on-the-job performance.

TEXT-DEPENDENT QUESTIONS

1. ***What are some of the military-specific tasks required of these jobs?***
2. ***What special training is required?***
3. ***What are some related, nonmilitary jobs?***

RESEARCH PROJECTS

1. ***Join a student trooper program. Find out if your school or local police force offers training programs for high school students.***
2. ***Find out about the experiences of military police officers in memoirs, such as:*** **Patrolling Baghdad** ***by Mark DePue or*** **Warrior Police** ***by Gordon Cucullu.***

Food Service Specialist/Cook

7

Prepare and cook meals. Practice the culinary arts. Boost military morale.

WORDS TO UNDERSTAND

contract out: a term for hiring an outside firm to perform a particular job.

dietetic: relating to special diets.

efficiently: working in a well-organized way, without wasted effort.

offset: to counteract the effect of something.

It is easy to forget, but food preparation is a crucial military job. After all, soldiers and sailors have to eat. As Napoleon Bonaparte famously said, "an army travels on its stomach." Some U.S. military kitchens serve thousands of meals at a time, while others prepare food for small groups. Food service specialists operate kitchen and dining facilities. They prepare all types of food. They also order and inspect food supplies. If you enjoy the culinary arts and possess excellent organizational and people skills, then a food service specialist might be the career field for you.

◀ **Culinary specialists prepare food at the Naval Medical Center in San Diego.**

Is This Job Right for You?

Would working as a food service specialist be a good fit for you? To find out, read each of the following questions and answer "Yes" or "No."

Yes *No* 1. *Are you interested in cooking and food preparation?*

Yes *No* 2. *Do you have high standards of personal cleanliness?*

Yes *No* 3. *Do you have an interest in nutrition and health?*

Yes *No* 4. *Can you understand and follow basic instructions easily?*

Yes *No* 5. *Do you like to work with your hands?*

Yes *No* 6. *Does the idea of feeding others give you pleasure?*

Yes *No* 7. *Are you good at math (for recipe conversions)?*

Yes *No* 8. *Can you work well as part of a team?*

Yes *No* 9. *Can you work* **efficiently** *under pressure?*

Yes *No* 10. *Can you stand on your feet all day if necessary?*

If you answered "Yes" to most of these questions, you might consider a career as a food service specialist. To find out more about this job, read on.

What's the Work Like?

As a food service specialist, you would be responsible for the preparation and service of food on the battlefield or back at the base. This means that you would need to estimate food requirements, and then order, receive, inspect, and store meat, fish, fruit, and vegetables. Menus would have to be prepared, budgets arranged and followed, and records carefully kept.

Your most important duty would be to feed service members. You'd measure, mix, prepare, and cook ingredients according to recipes. Of course, this would require

TALKING MONEY

The federal government pay scale starts low and ends low but includes excellent benefits. Base salary is $20,000 or less for the first two years of service. Military benefits include career training, health care, and money for college. In civilian life, the wages of cooks vary greatly. According to the U.S. Bureau of Labor Statistics, the mean annual salary for chefs and head cooks in 2016 was $43,180, while food preparation workers in places like schools, hospitals, and similar cafeterias averaged about $21,440 per year.

the knowledge of equipment such as ovens, broilers, grills, slicers, and blenders, and an understanding of the use of a variety of cutlery and pots and pans. During all food prep, you would make sure to follow proper procedures, cooking times, and temperatures. When the food is finally prepared and served, you would supervise or carry out general housekeeping duties; after all, the mess in the kitchen has to be cleaned up when the meal is over.

In the old days, military meals consisted of one or two entrées with vegetables. For breakfast, the only choices were scrambled eggs, cereal, bacon, and toast. There were few healthy choices and no junk food. Those days are long gone. Today, most dining facilities give the choice of a full meal with multiple entrées, including burgers, hot dogs, sandwiches, fries, and chicken. For individuals concerned with health and nutrition, there is usually a "healthy-heart" menu and a salad bar. For breakfast, a service member can choose anything from a small fruit cup to a huge made-to-order omelet with side dishes.

Of course, if a service member is in combat, he or she does not have time for a sit-down meal. In this case, he or she eats an individual MRE (meal, ready-to-eat), a self-contained meal that provides all the nutrition a service member on a mission needs.

▲ **A navy culinary specialist prepares dinner.**

Whether you are on a submarine, an air base, or in a combat zone, your skills in preparing food would not only feed people but also help to maintain the morale of your fellow service members.

Who's Hiring?

- Obviously, everyone in the U.S. armed forces has to eat. All branches need food service specialists.
- Contract operations. The U.S. armed forces now **contracts out** many dining facilities to private, nonmilitary companies. At large installations, the cooks are usually civilians employed by contractors. There are still openings for military "cooks," but there is a definite trend toward outsourcing.

TALKING TRENDS

The number of food service specialists depends on the size of the military. This can vary widely from year to year. When the U.S. military is fighting a war overseas, the need for food service specialists obviously increases, but private contracting offsets the number of food specialist positions. However, even with outsourcing, there should always be opportunities for military cooks. In civilian life, job openings for chefs, cooks, and food preparation workers are expected to be much in demand through 2024.

Where Are the Jobs?

Food service specialists work in just about every duty station available throughout the United States and various locations overseas. Food service specialists can be found in a number of different settings. You may be responsible for cooking or supervising kitchen workers in dining halls, hospitals, field kitchens, or aboard a ship. You might work in refrigerated meat lockers. Occasionally, you'd work outdoors in tents while preparing and serving food under field conditions. A navy cook might cook on a ship's deck for a barbecue known as a "steel beach picnic." Other military cooks prepare meals for dignitaries and other distinguished guests when visiting other countries.

Military food service specialists usually work in clean, well-ventilated, and decently lit kitchens and dining facilities. Most military kitchens have modern equipment, convenient work areas, and some even have air-conditioning. Obviously, conditions in the field or in combat zones are less than ideal, and working conditions can vary dramatically. Food service specialists usually share small spaces with hot stoves and ovens. They are under constant pressure to prepare meals quickly, yet ensure that quality is maintained and safety and sanitation guidelines are observed.

▲ Members of the U.S. Air Force prepare meals in a field kitchen.

A Typical Day

Here are some highlights for a typical day as a food service specialist.

Check inventory and order supplies. If you're cooking omelets for 350 soldiers, you had better make sure you have enough eggs, or some troops will be very unhappy.

Prepare the meal. Cooks cook; it's that simple. You may prepare omelets, cook waffles, pancakes, and grits. Other meals may include steaks, chops, and roasts, or you may bake or fry chicken, turkey, and fish. You might also prepare gravies and sauces and bake breads, cakes, pies, and pastries.

Supervise clean up. You probably won't have to scrub out the pots, but it's your job to make sure they are all clean and sanitary. Ovens, stoves, mixers, and utensils all have to be spotless. Food poisoning could incapacitate a whole platoon.

See what it's like to be a military chef.

NOTES FROM THE FIELD

Food services supervisor, *USS Wadsworth*

Q: *How did you get your job?*

A: **I joined the navy right after high school to travel and to learn a trade. After spending part of my first tour as a seaman apprentice working in the mess hall, I discovered that cooking was what I wanted to do. My first assignment was on the USS *Waldron* in Norfolk, Virginia, where I worked in the ship's galley.**

Q: *What do you like best about your job?*

A: **I have spent the past several years as a food services supervisor on different ships and have done what I wanted to do—learn to cook and travel around the world.**

Q: *What's the most challenging part of your job?*

A: **[As a] senior chef on the USS *New Orleans*, I managed a 35-person staff that fed 580 crew members and, at times, 1,800 marines (nearly 7,000 meals a day).**

Q: *What are the keys to success in being a food service specialist?*

A: **Through the navy, I went to cooking school to learn more about menu planning, nutrition, and cooking skills. After cooking school, my career really took off. . . . I was assigned to the USS *O'Callahan* to be in charge of running the entire mess. At that time, I was also promoted to chief petty officer. The most important day of my career was the day that I put on the hat, signifying that I had become a chef.**

Start Preparing Now

- Take relevant classes in high school. Helpful school subjects include cooking classes, nutrition and related classes, health, mathematics, accounting, and chemistry.
- Take a specialized course. Community colleges and vocational schools offer specialized classes in cooking and food service.
- Get some experience. Most fast-food or short-order cooks require little education or training; most skills are learned on the job. The more experience you have, the more it will help you in this field.

Training and How to Get It

Job training for a food service specialist begins with nine weeks of basic training. Even food service specialists must learn basic soldiering skills. This is followed by about 10 weeks of advanced individual training, including practice in food preparation. The length of your training depends on your particular job specialty. Part of this time will be spent in the classroom and part in on-the-job training in the kitchen.

As a food service specialist, you'll study standard and **dietetic** menus and recipes and food preparation. You'll also learn related skills, such as how to order food and supplies, how to properly use and care for kitchen equipment, and how to store perishable food items. Other subjects include the safe use of equipment, recipe conversions, basic food preparation terminology, and sanitation.

At first, you'll prepare ingredients and cook basic dishes under the supervision of experienced cooks. You'll probably be responsible for maintaining the kitchen in a clean, orderly fashion. Over time, your responsibilities will expand, and soon you will be cooking for hundreds.

Food service specialists may branch out into other areas beyond culinary arts. After initial study, you can acquire further training in accounting, administration and management,

▲ **A chef gives pizza dough rolling tips to a culinary specialist aboard a guided-missile destroyer.**

nutritional cooking, dining facility management, and entertainment services. You might also study computer accounting and inventory software in order to better keep track of the vast quantities of food used by the military. Some of your formal and on-the-job training will transfer to college credit hours. You can use this credit toward an associate's or bachelor's degree.

Learn the Lingo

Here are a few words you'll hear in this career:

- **Cambro** A large plastic pan used for storage. The term comes from the company that makes these containers. They are also referred to as a Lexan, a name taken from a competing company.
- **DFAC** Abbreviation for "dining facilities administration center," in other words, a cafeteria or mess hall.
- **Galley** The area on a ship where meals are prepared.
- **KP** Short for "kitchen patrol." This is a one-day duty assignment for soldiers to do mess hall work. They might help prepare food, clean out grease traps, or most famously, peel potatoes.
- **Mess** A meal.

Finding a Job

Many young men and women enlist in the armed forces right out of high school. At 18 years old you can sign up on your own; if you're 17, you can do so with a parent's permission.

To serve in the U.S. military, a person must pass physical requirements and a background check. For the army, your service obligations would be determined at the recruiter's office. You can agree with the recruiter to serve for two, three, four, or even five years. (Read the fine print of your service contract carefully before you agree to sign anything to understand your proposed length of service and number of tours of duty.)

In civilian life, cooks' jobs are frequently advertised in newspapers and on the Web. Because turnover is high in entry-level positions, the best source may be word-of-mouth.

Tips for Success

- Have a thick skin. No matter how well you cook, it's traditional for service members to complain about the food. You will have to get used to the griping and just deal with it.

▲ **Sometimes, military culinary specialists take part in cooking competitions. Here, the Navy's culinary team practices making an entrée at Fort Lee.**

- There's no place like the U.S. armed services for a diverse population. You may have the opportunity to learn a lot about cuisines from many cultures—and this could propel you toward a career of cooking if you decide to pursue one.

Reality Check

A career as a cook can get stale quickly. You're standing for hours at a time, lifting heavy pots and pans, and working around hot ovens and grills. Be prepared to do a lot of sweating. Also, if you want to cook for servicemen and -women, consider applying directly with a food-service contractor, such as KBR (formerly Kellogg, Brown and Root). You won't need to make as lengthy of a commitment.

Some Other Jobs to Think About

Cook. If you can get the experience or training out of the military, there are thousands of job possibilities in the civilian world.

Restaurant owner. If you are an entrepreneur with access to start-up money, you can own your own business.

Caterer. This food service specialty combines cooking with entrepreneurship. You'll get to serve more interesting food than in the military.

LEARN MORE ONLINE

CAREERS IN THE MILITARY

This Web site is the starting point for any investigation of jobs in the armed forces. It includes many useful job descriptions and links. http://www.careersinthemilitary.com

TODAY'S MILITARY

This site gives in-depth information on each branch of the U.S. armed forces. http://www.todaysmilitary.com

THE AMERICAN CULINARY FEDERATION (ACF)

With more than 17,000 members, ACF is the main professional chefs' organization in North America. This Web site has information on apprenticeship and certification programs and a career center. http://www.acfchefs.org

NATIONAL RESTAURANT ASSOCIATION

This Web site includes a directory of two- and four-year colleges that offer food service career courses. http://www.restaurant.org

How to Move Up

- Advance in the military. In the armed forces, promotions can come quickly based on time in service and merit. After seven years, you can become a chef. Chefs plan and prepare food menus and recipes and direct kitchen staff. After 15 years, you can advance as high as food service supervisor. These officers plan budgets, monitor food service expenses, and determine personnel, equipment, and food supply needs.
- Advance in civilian life. The skills you learn as a food service specialist will allow you to work in civilian restaurants, cafeterias, hotels, hospitals, manufacturing plants, schools, and other organizations that have their own dining facilities. You can advance by taking classes at a technical school or two-year college to specialize in desserts, advanced cooking techniques, cooking for banquets or parties, and cooking styles from around the world. The American Culinary Federation accredits a variety of different training programs and sponsors apprenticeship programs around the country.

TEXT-DEPENDENT QUESTIONS

1. *What are some of the tasks performed by food service specialists?*
2. *What special training is needed?*
3. *What does "KP" stand for?*
4. *What are some related jobs you might consider?*

RESEARCH PROJECTS

1. *There are thousands of shelters and soup kitchens serving meals to the needy every day, and they can all use volunteers. It's a great way to find out if you'd enjoy cooking for large groups of people while helping out your community as well.*
2. *Take charge of making a dinner for your family, including planning the meal, figuring out what groceries you need, preparing the food, and, importantly, taking charge of the cleanup afterward.*

BLEED
AIR

Aircraft Mechanic

8

Keep planes safely airborne.
Solve complex mechanical problems.
Work with cutting-edge equipment.

WORDS TO UNDERSTAND

powerplant: another term for an aircraft engine.

preventive: describes steps taken ahead of time to avoid (prevent) future problems.

Does the idea of working with some of the world's most high-tech aircraft and equipment sound cool? As a military aircraft mechanic, you would tinker with the newest electronics and repair aircraft so that they remain safe and ready to fly. The U.S. military uses a wide range of helicopters and airplanes to move people and equipment during military operations. Countless military missions depend on aircraft for patrol, transport, and flight training. Not a single helicopter, jet fighter, or cargo plane leaves the runway or the flight deck without the support of well-trained aircraft mechanics.

◀ An aviation mechanic inspects an aircraft engine.

Is This Job Right for You?

Would working as an aircraft mechanic be a good fit for you? To find out, read each of the following questions and answer "Yes" or "No."

Yes	*No*	**1.** *Do you like using your hands and power tools?*
Yes	*No*	**2.** *Do you have an interest in working with aircraft?*
Yes	*No*	**3.** *Could you deal with the pressure of making life-and-death repairs?*
Yes	*No*	**4.** *Do you possess good communication skills?*
Yes	*No*	**5.** *Do you have a good memory?*
Yes	*No*	**6.** *Are you interested in engine mechanics?*
Yes	*No*	**7.** *Do you have excellent problem-solving skills?*
Yes	*No*	**8.** *Can you understand and process new information?*
Yes	*No*	**9.** *Do you like taking classes in mathematics and shop mechanics?*
Yes	*No*	**10.** *Do you quickly comprehend what you have read?*

If you answered "Yes" to most of these questions, you might consider a career as an aircraft mechanic. To find out more about this job, read on.

What's the Work Like?

Military aircraft mechanics inspect, service, and repair helicopters and airplanes. However, as an aircraft mechanic, you will have a range of career subspecialties. Aircraft are very complex machines composed of many different systems that need frequent servicing. You might work on specific types of aircraft, such as jets, propeller planes, or helicopters. Or you might specialize in one section of a particular type of aircraft, such as the engine or electrical system.

TALKING MONEY

Privates and corporals, with between one and four years' experience, respectively, draw base annual salaries of $19,000 and $29,000. Benefits packages for military personnel are excellent and include career training, health care, tuition support, and life insurance. Most soldiers on active duty also receive a housing allowance, a subsistence allowance, combat pay, and other benefits. In civilian life, the average annual salary for aircraft mechanics is about $61,000, according to 2016 data from the U.S. Bureau of Labor Statistics.

Airframe mechanics work on any part of the aircraft except the instruments, **power-plants**, and propellers. Powerplant mechanics work on engines and perform some work on propellers. Airframe-and-powerplant mechanics (A&P mechanics) work on all parts of the plane except the instruments. The majority of mechanics working on civilian aircraft are A&P mechanics. In the military, however, most aircraft mechanics specialize on very particular types of planes.

Some aircraft mechanics concentrate on repairing electrical systems. Instruments, lights, weapons, ignition systems, and landing gear all use electricity. If something is defective, such as a generator or wiring, mechanics repair or replace it. The increasing use of technology has led to more mechanics working on repairing electronic systems, such as computerized controls and radar systems. However, structural mechanics repair and replace nonelectric parts, such as bulkheads, beams, and aircraft skin.

▲ **Aviation structural mechanics prepare a fighter aircraft for a mission.**

Many aircraft mechanics specialize in **preventive** maintenance. They inspect engines, brakes, valves, pumps, and air-conditioning systems to make sure they are in good working order. These mechanics repair and replace worn or defective parts and keep records related to the maintenance. For example, a typical C-5 cargo plane requires about 20 hours of maintenance for every hour of flying time.

Whether specializing in electronics, hydraulics, engines, maintenance, or any other field, aircraft mechanics must test the equipment

TALKING TRENDS

The U.S. military depends on airpower, so there are always opportunities for aircraft mechanics. Civilian airports, airline companies, aircraft manufacturers, and government and law enforcement agencies also need aircraft mechanics. The Bureau of Labor Statistics estimates that jobs for aircraft mechanics will hold steady in the coming years: on the one hand, air travel is expected to increase, meaning more repairs will be needed; on the other hand, aircraft are becoming increasingly automated and may need fewer people to maintain them.

▲ **Aircraft mechanics perform tactical maintenance on a fighter jet.**

to make sure that it works properly after they repair it. They work as quickly as safety permits so that the aircraft can return to service without delay. In this way, an aircraft mechanic's skills are vital to the successful operation of the U.S. military.

Who's Hiring?

- Army
- Navy
- Air force
- Marine corps
- Coast guard

Where Are the Jobs?

Most military aircraft mechanics may be stationed anywhere around the world. You may work on a base in the United States, on the flight deck of an aircraft carrier off the coast of Lebanon, or on an island in the Pacific.

▲ **An aviation structural mechanic replaces a tail disconnect on a Sea Hawk helicopter.**

NOTES FROM THE FIELD

Assistant manager, *F-15 maintenance unit, U.S. Pacific Command, Camp H.M. Smith, Hawaii*

Q: ***How did you get your job?***

A: **After basic training, I went to aircraft mechanic's school and field training. After two years of performing unscheduled maintenance (pilot-reported problems) [at Andrews Airforce Base], I went to Goose Bay, Canada, for another field training course on the F-102 aircraft.**

Q: ***What do you like best about your job?***

A: **I saw the air force as a chance to get ahead and establish a good career, but it was having a job I really liked and being able to fly as well that really sold me.**

Q: ***What's the most challenging part of your job?***

A: **[It was serving] as the Pacific Air Force Command manager for several types of aircraft, ensuring that materials and supplies reached air force units in the Pacific. I . . . also [helped manage] a maintenance unit capable of supporting F-15 fighters anywhere in the world.**

Q: ***What are the keys to success to your job?***

A: **[You need to be very] mechanically inclined.**

Aircraft mechanics work in aircraft hangars and machine shops located on air bases or aboard aircraft carriers. Although mechanics usually work indoors, they sometimes work outdoors when hangars are full or when repairs must be made quickly.

Being an aircraft mechanic is a stressful job. Mechanics often work under time pressure to maintain flight schedules; long hours are a frequent problem, particularly in combat situations. They also have a tremendous responsibility to maintain safety standards. Millions of dollars of equipment, and more importantly, people's lives, depend on their skill and careful work.

The job has some physical drawbacks. Aircraft mechanics often examine engines by working through specially designed openings while standing on ladders or scaffolds or by using hoists or lifts to remove the entire engine from the craft. Mechanics must lift or pull heavy objects. They often stand, lie, or kneel in awkward positions. Noise and vibration are a constant problem when testing engines. However, wherever you work, you will never question the importance of your job. Every aircraft you take care of has to perform its mission successfully and return home safely.

A Typical Day

Here are some highlights for a typical day as an aircraft mechanic, who is specializing in electrical repair.

Perform preflight inspections. You are responsible for maintaining a squadron of wide-bodied C-5 cargo planes, performing daily preflight, and postflight aircraft inspections.

Rely on inspection equipment. A pilot reports that his left engine doesn't sound right. You use your skills to help take apart the engine and repair or replace parts. To do this you use precision instruments. You're measuring parts for wear and using X-ray and magnetic inspection equipment to check for invisible cracks.

Troubleshoot. During a preflight check, a pilot discovers that her aircraft's fuel gauge doesn't work. To solve the problem, you'll have to troubleshoot the electrical system. You use electrical test equipment to make sure that no wires are broken or shorted out. You discover the defective component and replace it.

Find out more about aircraft structural maintenance.

Start Preparing Now

- Take relevant classes in high school. Courses in math, physics, chemistry, electronics, computer science, and mechanical drawing are helpful because they incorporate many of the principles involved in the operation of aircraft. Knowledge of these principles is often necessary to make repairs.
- Take a course at a community college or vocational school. It never hurts to have as much specific training as possible.
- Learn to fly a plane. You can take classes at your local airfield. It is obviously much easier to understand the field if you have your pilot's license.

Training and How to Get It

Job training for an aircraft mechanic in the armed forces usually consists of about two months of basic training followed by anywhere from 14 to 52 weeks of advanced training. There are numerous subspecialties within aircraft repair and maintenance. Your length of training depends on which subspecialty you choose or are assigned.

The training you will receive will be a mixture of hands-on experience and classroom study. Some of the skills you might learn include engine disassembly and repair; the inspection and repair of hydraulic, fuel, and electrical systems; and the repair of aluminum, steel, and fiberglass airframes and coverings.

Apprentice military aircraft mechanics work under close supervision and perform routine repair and maintenance duties. They also keep maintenance logs in which any service or repairs are recorded. As new and more complex aircraft are designed, mechanics need ongoing training to update their skills. Most of the training you will receive can be counted toward credit hours for a vocational certificate, as well as toward a college degree.

In civilian life, most aircraft mechanics learn their job in one of about 170 trade schools certified by the Federal Aviation Administration (FAA). About one-third of these schools award two-year and four-year degrees in avionics or aviation technology. FAA training standards are established by law. They require that certified mechanic schools offer students a minimum of 1,900 actual class hours. Coursework in schools normally lasts from 18 to 24 months.

Some aircraft mechanics in the armed forces acquire enough general experience to satisfy the work experience requirements for an FAA certificate. With additional study, they may pass the certifying exam. In general, however, jobs in the military services are too specialized to provide the broad experience required by the FAA. Most armed forces mechanics have to complete the entire training program, although it is possible to receive some credit for the material they learned in the service.

Learn the Lingo

Here are a few words you'll hear in this career:

- **Drag** A force, such as air resistance, that slows an object in motion through the air.
- **FOD** An abbreviation for "foreign object damage." Jet engines can suffer major damage when an engine sucks up a rock on the runway or a bird in flight. FOD also includes hail, ice, dust, tools, bolts, and metal shavings. FOD causes damage worth an estimated $4 billion every year.

▲ A petty officer maintains the search and rescue crane on a Sea Hawk helicopter.

- **Hangar queen** An aircraft with a bad maintenance record that spends a great deal of time being repaired or maintained. Hangar queens are often pirated for spare parts for other aircraft.
- **Longeron** In aircraft construction, a longeron is a thin strip of wood or metal, to which the skin of the aircraft is fastened. Longerons are attached to frames (known as formers) in the case of the fuselage, or ribs in the case of a wing.

Finding a Job

Many young men and women enlist in the armed forces right out of high school. An 18-year-old high school graduate can walk into the local recruiter's office and enlist. Seventeen-year-olds can also enlist but need a parent's permission.

To serve in the U.S. military, a person must pass physical requirements and a background check. Academically, an applicant must score at least a 31 on the Armed Forces Qualification Test (AFQT). For the army, your service obligations would be determined at the recruiter's office. You can agree with the recruiter to serve for two, three, four, or even five years. (Read the fine print of your service contract carefully before you agree to sign anything to understand your potential length of service or number of tours of duty.)

For a civilian aircraft mechanic job, military experience is a great advantage when seeking employment. Employers consider applicants with formal training to be the most desirable. In addition, many people in the civilian aviation field have a military background. Jobs are advertised on the Web and with training programs.

Tips for Success

- Small errors can be fatal. Aircraft mechanics need an almost obsessive concern with details. A leftover pile of metal shavings in an engine can disable a $200 million plane.
- Though machines are your focus, people are the most important part of your job. Share information, develop contacts for the future, and learn different styles of getting things done.

Reality Check

If you are hoping to convert directly to a civilian career, you may be disappointed. Few aircraft mechanics in the armed forces acquire enough general experience to satisfy the requirements for an FAA certificate.

Some Other Jobs to Think About

Engineer. Workers in engineering use their analytical skills to solve practical problems. In this occupation, you are not restricted to aircraft.

Machinist. In this position, you can make, repair, and modify metal and nonmetal parts for engines and other types of machines.

Carpenter, electrician, plumber. These are all construction positions that involve problem-solving repairs.

How to Move Up

- Advance in the military. In the armed forces, promotions can come quickly based on time in service and merit. Advanced level aircraft mechanics supervise and train other service members. After 19 years, you can advance as high as aircraft maintenance supervisor. These officers are in charge of large aircraft maintenance and repair facilities. They also plan and direct inspection, service, and modification of aircraft.
- Advance in civilian life. The skills you learn as a military aircraft mechanic will help prepare you to work for aircraft manufacturers, commercial airlines, and government agencies. Opportunities are plentiful for this type of work, but you may have to complete a formal training program. Classes and programs at FAA-certified trade schools will give you the necessary credentials to advance in avionics, aviation technology, or aviation maintenance management.

LEARN MORE ONLINE

CAREERS IN THE MILITARY

This Web site is the starting point for any investigation of jobs in the armed forces. It includes many useful job descriptions and links.
http://www.careersinthemilitary.com

TODAY'S MILITARY

This site gives in-depth information on each branch of the U.S. armed forces.
http://www.todaysmilitary.com

FEDERAL AVIATION ADMINISTRATION: MECHANICS

This Web site contains more than 20 links to information about licenses, regulations, training, policies, technical information, and forms.
http://www.faa.gov/mechanics

TEXT-DEPENDENT QUESTIONS

1. *What's the average annual salary for an aircraft mechanic in civilian life?*
2. *What's a "hangar queen" good for?*
3. *A typical C-5 cargo plane requires how many hours of maintenance for every hour of flying time?*

RESEARCH PROJECTS

1. *Find out more about the FAA's rigorous standards for airplane mechanics by exploring their site (https://www.faa.gov/mechanics/become/basic/). By following the links, you'll also be able to download their handbooks and manuals.*
2. *There aren't tons of opportunities for hobbyist plane mechanics, but if there does happen to be a small airstrip in your community, stop by and introduce yourself; you might be able to get a tour. If not, you can start smaller by working on car engines or even fixing your lawnmower. The point is to start getting hands-on experience anywhere you can.*

▲ The planes you service may be used to transport people or equipment.

INDEX

PHOTO CREDITS

Cover

(Central image) U.S. Air Force/Beau Wade; (top to bottom) U.S. Army, U.S. Air Force, U.S. Navy photo/Mass Communication Specialist 2nd Class Eddie Harrison, U.S. Air Force, U.S. Air Force/ Senior Airman Andrew Lee

Interior

4 (left to right), U.S. Army; U.S. Air Force photo by Senior Airman Carlin Leslie; U.S. Navy photo by Mass Communication Specialist 2nd Class Eddie Harrison; U.S. Air Force photo; U.S. Air Force photo by Senior Airman Andrew Lee; 11, Steve Debenport/iStock; 12, By US Air Force from USA/ WIKI; 14, By US Air Force from USA/WIKI; 16, By US Air Force from USA/WIKI; 18, U.S. Air Force photo by Staff Sgt. William P.Coleman; 21, U.S. Air Force photo by Senior Airman Elizabeth Van Patten; 25, U.S. Air Force photo/Airman 1st Class Cory W. Bush; 26, U.S. Army; 29, U.S. Navy photo by Mass Communication Specialist 3rd Class Will Tyndall; 31, U.S. Air Force photo/Senior Airman Brett Clashman; 35, U.S. Air Force photo by Senior Airman Tristin English; 37, U.S. Navy photo by Mass Communication Specialist 3rd Class Shawn J. Stewart; 38, U.S. Air Force photo by/Master Sgt. Jeromy K. Cross; 41, U.S. Air Force Photo by Staff Sgt. Joshua Garcia; 43, U.S. Air Force photo; 45, U.S. Air Force photo by Senior Airman Peter Reft; 50, U.S. Navy photo by Mass Communication Specialist 3rd Class Raul Moreno Jr.; 53, U.S. Army; 55, U.S. Army photo by Pfc. Jasmine N. Walthall; 58, U.S. Air Force photo; 60, U.S. Air Force photo by Staff Sgt. Natasha Stannard; 62, mady70/iStock; 65, By U.S. Navy photo by Mass Communication Specialist 2nd Class Julian R. Moorefield/WIKI; 66, Navy photo by Petty Officer 2nd Class Sean M. Castellano; 67, U.S. Navy photo; 70, U.S. Navy photo by Mass Communication Specialist 2nd Class Wilyanna Harper; 74, By US Air Force from USA/WIKI; 77, U.S. Navy photo by Lt. Cmdr. Corey Barker; 79 (UP), U.S. Coast Guard; 79 (LO), U.S. Department of Defense; 81, By US Air Force from USA/WIKI; 85, U.S. Navy photo by Mass Communication Specialist 2nd Class John Philip Wagner Jr.; 89, U.S. Navy photo by Mass Communication Specialist 2nd Class Bryan M. Ilyankoff; 91, U.S. Air Force photo by Master Sgt. Shane A. Cuomo; 93, U.S. Navy photo by Mass Communication Specialist 1st Class John Parker; 95, By Official U.S. Navy Page from United States of America/WIKI; 98, By U.S. Navy photo by Mass Communication Specialist 2nd Class Cayman Santoro/WIKI; 101, U.S. Navy photo by Mass Communication Specialist 3rd Class Karl Anderson; 102, U.S. Air Force photo by Staff Sgt. David Miller; 103, U.S. Navy photo by Mass Communication Specialist 2nd Class Charlotte C. Oliver; 107, Navy photo by Seaman Kennishah J. Maddux; 110, U.S. Air Force photo by Staff Sgt. Darnell T. Cannady